THE MINISTER
AS DIAGNOSTICIAN

THE MINISTER
AS DIAGNOSTICIAN

Personal Problems
in Pastoral Perspective

PAUL W. PRUYSER

THE WESTMINSTER PRESS
PHILADELPHIA

BOOK DESIGN BY DOROTHY E. JONES

PUBLISHED BY THE WESTMINSTER PRESS®
PHILADELPHIA, PENNSYLVANIA

PRINTED IN THE UNITED STATES OF AMERICA

6

Library of Congress Cataloging in Publication Data

Pruyser, Paul W
　The minister as diagnostician.

　Includes bibliographical references and index.
　1. Pastoral theology.　2. Pastoral psychology.
3. Clergy—Office.　I.　Title.
BV4011.P7　　　253　　　76–8922
ISBN 0–664–24123–9

TO THE MEMORY OF
THOMAS W. KLINK
COLLEAGUE AND FRIEND

CONTENTS

want precisely their pastors, rather than some other specialists, to guide them in their search for a self-diagnosis? What
if they want to place themselves in a pastoral-theological
rather than a medical, psychiatric, legal, or social perspective?
What if they want to be in several professional hands at one
and the same time? To heed those desires would make the
pastor a diagnostician in his own (and his client's) right. And
to foster his client's need for self-evaluation would make the
pastor a diagnostician of a special kind, using a conceptual
system and practical framework without equal among other
specialists in the helping professions.

The thesis of this book is that pastors, like all other
professional workers, possess a body of theoretical and
practical knowledge that is uniquely their own, evolved over
years of practice by themselves and their forebears. Adding
different bits of knowledge and techniques by borrowing
from other disciplines, such as psychiatry and psychology,
does not undo the integrity and usefulness of their own basic
and applied sciences. Adding clinical insights and skills to
their pastoral work does not—should not—shake the authenticity of their pastoral outlook and performance. Thus, with
this thesis, the book appeals to pastors to reflect on their
special heritage and use its theoretical foundations and
practical applications to the full. It is addressed to pastors in
any stage of their formation and growth, from seminary
students on to accomplished practitioners, and to their
various teachers, including those who, as in clinical pastoral
education, do their teaching in hospitals, clinics, prisons, etc.

The book grew naturally, though slowly and stepwise, out
of previous publications which had a more limited focus as
journal articles typically have. Teaching demands, consultation work, and the encouragement of colleagues and friends
conspired to turn me away from making sketches and start me
to do some painting on a fair-sized canvas. And now the time

has come to hang the painting on the wall, for display and critical appraisal. Only thus can I myself take distance from it for a good look.

Invited to give the Lowell Lectures at Boston University in the winter of 1975, I used portions of this book in my presentations.

I owe a special word of thanks to several pastors who were willing to share with me the pastoral case materials they had obtained under the influence of the contents of my manuscript. They were taken by its suggestions sufficiently to try their hand at putting my recommendations into practice and writing reports about their cases. Five of these reports are included in Chapter X. Though these pastors merit to be named and publicly thanked for their work, they agreed to remain anonymous in order to protect the confidentiality of their parishioners' trust in them.

As always, Dr. Seward Hiltner of Princeton Theological Seminary let me benefit from his incisive critique. Mrs. Kathleen Bryan took competent care of the manuscript in its various stages. I thank her too. And I am grateful to the staff of The Westminster Press, whose editorial comments and recommendations did much to improve the early version of this work.

On the dedication page·I have commemorated not only a man, a skillful pastoral practitioner and a leader in the clinical pastoral education movement, but a friend over whose untimely death many of us still sorrow.

P.W.P.

1

PROFESSIONAL KNOWLEDGE
AS PERSPECTIVE

In his philosophical novel *Nausea*,[1] Sartre introduces a rather weird figure whom he calls the Self-Taught Man. He can be found every day in the city library, reading book after book while nibbling on a chocolate bar. If one would watch him closely for a number of days or weeks, one would find him taking one book after another from the stacks in alphabetical order. He is now near the end of "L"; soon he will start taking the "M's." He teaches himself alphabetically, in the apparent conviction that knowledge is cumulative and that learning is a matter of assiduously taking note of everything from A to Z. As Sartre portrays him, the Self-Taught Man's intellectual curiosity is in part driven by a perverse sexual urge: along with his reading, he seeks opportunities for sensuously stroking the hands of young boys under the library table.

The belief that knowledge is additive, that its acquisition is a matter of plowing through everything knowable, is not confined to a few eccentric loners. Sadly, even in ivy-clad halls of learning there are students, and perhaps an occasional faculty member, who seem to think that all knowledge is of the same order and that he who knows five things is vastly superior to the man who knows only three. On these grounds, curricula are forever swelling. If theology is a good thing to teach in a seminary, theology plus sociology is better, and theology plus sociology plus psychology superlative. Like the gross national product, knowledge is subjected to the indiscriminate, voracious demands of "more"!

The addiction to "more" in knowledge and curriculum offerings can lead to an interesting variant of the Self-Taught Man. Imagine a novice sausage maker who is trying to press too much meat into one good-sized skin. Having put all his bologna into the skin, he is now stuffing it with liverwurst, pressing on firmly so as to get in his several pounds of pepperoni also. As a result of his pressureful stuffing, the closed end of the skin bursts, and our fledgling sausage maker may simply end up with pepperoni, while the bologna and liverwurst have fallen to the floor. This meaty analogy serves to suggest another academic hazard: the theology student who eliminates his theology while he is studying sociology will soon expel both when he stuffs himself full of psychology courses. In this succession, knowledge is no longer additive or cumulative, but seriate. For every new thing learned, something old is forgotten—consciousness functions like a container of limited size, whose content must be kept as homogeneous as possible.

If the Self-Taught Man could come to Whitehead's *Adventures of Ideas*[2] and *Process and Reality*,[3] which would unfortunately be near the end of the alphabet in an author file, by which time he would probably be in his eighties, he might come to see that knowledge is not additive nor cumulative. He would find that it is pluralistic and perspectival. It consists of "prehensions" of fleeting, specific "concrescences" which are, as it were, way stations of thought rather than finished edifices. He would find that thought must be open-ended because reality is constantly reshaping itself, or that our reality picture must be open-ended because human thought is constantly reshaping itself.

Though one may at first be put off by Whitehead's odd and somewhat ponderous words, his thoughts should be heeded because they address an issue that professional persons, particularly those in the helping professions, encounter almost daily. What professional helper has not been in meetings of different experts trying to size up somebody's problem, in an effort to give help or make a constructive intervention? Say a family with a working mother, an unemployed father, and several children, one of whom has had a first light brush with the law, has just been evicted from its rented home. Sooner or later the meeting becomes a debate when one of the prospective helpers asks, What is the *real* problem? And then, without waiting for the others to answer, he proceeds to push for his own viewpoint. The social worker politely hears out the lawyer and the minister who are involved in the case, but insists that the real problem is the culture of poverty in which this family has found itself for years. If a psychiatrist were present, he might focus on the husband's extraordinary dependency on his sturdy, mothering wife who holds everything precariously together, but at an emotional price for the children, especially the boys who have a poor identification model in the father. To the psychiatrist, the real problem lies in the mixed-up emotions attached to the confused, and sometimes reversed, roles in this family. If the company included a priest who had known this family for some time and heard the father's occasional confessions, the real problem might turn out to be the husband's marital infidelity and the moral laxity that has come to prevail in this family. The priest sees in this sinful fact the real problem. And so on.

For all human misfortunes, difficulties, mishaps, or symptoms presented to the various helping professions, how does one find out what the problem is? How can one sort out the various formulations offered so as to spot the *real* problem? Does not each discipline or profession find its problem definition real? Is the definition of problems offered by the strongest or most popular discipline at any given time the most real? If three or four different professionals disagree, is one profession supposed to win the argument for having given the "most real" definition? Is there some special expert about reality who can arbitrate such battles?

These are issues besetting the helping professions with which every pastor is familiar, although he may have given only furtive thought to them. The issues are painful if one would think them through, for they involve power relations between disciplines. The voices of some helpers get muffled by the louder voices of other helpers. One kind of professional judgment is forced to succumb to another kind of professional judgment. One helping relationship, though offered, is brushed aside in favor of another relationship, for reasons that may have more to do with the shifting patterns of the popular image of a discipline than with the pertinence of the adopted viewpoint.

Whitehead's position on knowledge, adapted to the professional issues I am raising, allows us to get beyond any form of one-upmanship between the professions. I believe that this is a great gain for interdisciplinary discourse and cooperation. All disciplines deal with reality. All helping professions are able to come up with definitions of the real problem. Disciplines and professions represent only so many different perspectives in which anything real can be grasped. Each perspective is partial, limited, specific—none is more real than another.

For the observations and arguments that are to follow, I will thus regard each science, each discipline, each branch of learning, each profession, each skill, each art as a special and unique perspective. Each is brought to bear upon the chaotic manifold of raw experience which William James once described as "one big blooming buzzing confusion." [4] Each *bit* of knowledge is then also a *form* of knowledge. It functions within a particular perspective, partakes of a special language game, and forms an integral part of a particular set of operations. The eventual integration of all these perspectives into one synthetic view may be a difficult philosophical problem in an era that does not recognize queens of sciences or master disciplines, since it is weary of intellectual authoritarianism. Still, selective integrations of a few well-chosen perspectives may be cautiously attempted—with the proper open-endedness and for circumscribed purposes.

I shall make a modest endeavor, not quite to integrate two different perspectives, but to bring them into thoughtful apposition to each other. My choices are theology and psychiatry—more specifically, pastoral theology and clinical psychiatry. Both of these perspectives are already blurred at the edges. Pastoral theology has already been greatly affected by psychiatric, medical, and psychological influences, whereas clinical psychiatry has received much input from biology, medicine, psychology, sociology, and the history of the cure of souls. At times, I may have to speak quite broadly of the "theological" and the "psychological" disciplines to acknowledge the intricate and unstable mixture of basic and applied sciences prevailing in each case, in which nevertheless a distinct focus can be discerned. At other times I shall refer to the specific basic, applied, or ancillary sciences, and the special techniques or skills that are historically associated with each of these perspectives, anchoring each in a special scholarly and professional tradition.

My choice of pastoral theology and clinical psychiatry is instigated by well-considered opportunism, paired with a

personal conviction. At the present time, these two disciplines have an explicitly holistic ambition. They constitute
broad views of human reality which do not leave out life's
untidy details and do not avoid man's rocky roads to
satisfaction in health or salvation. Both are attuned to the
professional value of helping, in several of its aspects: healing,
guiding, sustaining. Both disciplines are widely seen as
relevant to man's daily plight, and are endowed with an aura
of potency for bringing relief from undue stress and suffering.
Millions of people demand personal services from one or the
other, or from combinations of both. Both disciplines are
also beset by special problems that make their comparison
opportune: pastoral theology may contain much crypto-
psychology, and clinical psychiatry may contain much crypto-
theology.

The opportunistic note in my comparing the theological
and the psychological disciplines also derives from my own
professional situation. As a clinical psychologist I have had
occasion to mingle in two very different worlds, each quite
complex—the "theological" and the "psychiatric," both
terms taken in a generic sense. I am neither a theologian nor
a psychiatrist; I am neither a pastor nor a physician. My
particular interest is in personality theory, which is in
principle applicable to theological as well as psychiatric
thought, and pertinent to pastoral as well as clinical work. I
work in a psychiatric institution, where I am engaged not only
in clinical activities but also in clinically derived thinking and
clinically relevant instruction and writing. In that institution
I have for some time shouldered the responsibility for
professional training, that is, the graduate and postgraduate
education of professionals as diverse as psychiatrists, social
workers, psychologists, clergy, occupational therapists, nurses,
and medical students. My duties forced me to be aware of
differences and similarities between these professions, and to

be alert to the dangers of identity confusion to which students in a multidisciplinary setting can fall prey. But I have for various reasons also been engaged in seminary education, ranging from classroom teaching on psychological and psychiatric subjects to advising deans and faculty groups on ways of bringing psychological instruction to bear on training in pastoral care and counseling. The latter activity had clearly the nature of consultation work: I did not, on account of it, become a pastoral counselor. Nor did I become in any sense a theologian or a pastor in consultation work that I have done for church boards and agencies, or in being a board member of the erstwhile Council for Clinical Training.

The consultant's role in all these settings enhanced my curiosity about the complex worlds in which healers and helpers move. It gave me opportunity to learn something about how one profession borrows, absorbs, or assimilates knowledge and skill from another profession with ever-shifting patterns of give-and-take. The consultant sees diverse patterns of interaction between the disciplines. He sees "mixers" and purists; he sees people to whom the boundaries between disciplines are permeable and others to whom these remain formidable barriers. He finds some conceptions of professional identity rigidly anchored in traditional, never-changing patterns of knowledge and work, and others so fluid that identity confusion abounds.

Given these observations, the consultant's role is inevitably somewhat dialectical—he has to redress off-balance situations. He can be neither solely a lavish mixer nor a stingy purist. When he sees too much mixing and confusion he has to call attention to principles of professional specificity; when he sees too much purism he must argue for some give-and-take, to loosen up the rigidity. Throughout this book I will seek to maintain the position of a consultant, taking a

II

THE TOUCHSTONE OF
PROFESSIONAL INTEGRITY

To get a handle on the problem situation presented in the previous chapter, I propose a concise focus: the minister as diagnostician. This focus seems natural, logical, and pointed when one considers that all helpers have to address themselves to situations that need, in the first place, some kind of definition.

In what way, with what concepts, in what words, with what outlook does a practicing pastor assess the problem of a client who seeks his pastoral help? What, if anything, distinguishes a pastoral from a psychological assessment? What basic and applied sciences does a pastor use when he makes himself available to someone who seeks his help in solving some personal problem? In what terms does he describe his client and size up his problems? In making his pastoral help available, how does he proceed to heal, guide, or sustain the person who is turning to him for assistance? Does he make a prior evaluation, or does he just dash into certain helping routines which he has practiced? If he makes a diagnosis, how does he do so? And does his diagnosis have any bearing upon his helping moves, his counseling techniques or goals, his advice-giving, his encouragements, his pastoral interventions? Does he know what his clients seek of him, and does he realize what they hope to attain in selecting their pastor rather than a lawyer, doctor, or social worker as their prospective helper?

These are not spuriously abstract questions. Though they have much to do with theory, they are not merely academic. They have been forced upon my mind by diverse practical and theoretical considerations, in which the authenticity of various helping professions and the integrity of their disciplines have become important foci of concern. Let me share in greater detail and by vignettes of participatory observation some strands of professional experience gained over the years which have led to the questions I raised, and to my choice of diagnosis as a focus of concern.

I happened to enter my own profession in the exciting years following World War II, when clinical psychology, quickly merged with dynamic psychiatry, received much impetus from heavy demands for its services by victims of mental turmoil. An enlightened citizenry was demanding high-quality mental hospitals and clinics to replace the snake pits that had accumulated over the past fifty years. My profession also received impetus from progressive parents and educators seeking instruction in the rules of mental hygiene, from professional leaders ready to give advice and eager to prove their discipline's viability, and from increasingly available federal, state, and private money for services, research, and professional training. From the start, that "second psychiatric revolution" as it has been called (the first one was the discovery and early application of psychoanalysis), was attuned to interdisciplinary teamwork that triggered the modern pluralistic term "mental health professions." Among others, some ministers sought to be educated as mental hospital or prison chaplains, dealing with suffering people in crisis situations. Theological schools introduced courses into their curricula in psychopathology, dynamic psychiatry, human development, and counseling. The whole clinical pastoral education movement, already in operation for a few decades, underwent great expansion and formalization, becoming a popular adjunct, enrichment, or specialization for many pastors.

In those years I saw chaplains at work in the hospitals where I served. Many were utterly convinced that psychiatry and theology had much to offer to each other. Lunchtime and evening conversations led to many fascinating comparisons and intriguing debates. Jointly we taught in seminars for psychiatric residents, seminarians, or older parish pastors. I became aware that much of the instruction was one-sided, with the consent of both parties: the theologians sat at the feet of the psychiatric Gamaliels and seemed to like it, with only some occasional theological repartee.

Then came a second experience. I became engaged in consulting with theological schools about the place and form of the psychological disciplines in theological education. What should be emphasized, theory or practice? If both, in what proportions? I tried to help with the acquisition of well-trained teachers in these subjects who could handle case-study methods, provide skillful supervision, and act as gatekeepers to the world of psychiatric or medical ideas, manpower, institutions, and practices. Doing a good deal of extramural teaching myself, sitting on planning committees in seminaries, and watching the polite internecine warfare between faculty members in the systematic and those in the practical fields on the seminary campus, I sympathized with the difficult situation of the poor deans. I wrote tracts spelling it all out—what subjects to teach, how to reform traditional fieldwork, how to use supervision, what were the leading or promising psychiatric schools of thought, what should be done for continuing education of ministers, what were the blind alleys and the cutting edges for interdiscipli-

nary dialogue between theology and psychology, even to the
point of sorting out viable from ill-fated topics for doctoral
dissertations.

A third welter of experiences was thrust upon me when I
became director of professional education in a large psychiatric center well known for its dedication to the extended team
approach, in clinical practice as well as in training. I now had
to deal with the *specific* curricula for psychiatrists, nurses,
psychologists, clergymen, social workers, and others, as well as
the *joint* courses deemed suitable for all groups or for certain
combinations. I learned about vocational stress points and
career hazards in the various professions, and began to
surmise something about motives for career choice. In
addition, I learned that one cannot ignore the powerful
traditions and ethoses of the professions. I did some teaching
in nearly all programs, and got involved in supervision and
consultation, across disciplinary boundaries. Here again I
found for clergy a prevailing one-sided instruction—pastors
were eager to absorb as much psychological knowledge and
skill as they could, without even thinking of instructional
reciprocity. They rarely sought to teach the other professions
from their own basic disciplines or skills. Neither were they
asked for any kind of instruction by members of the other
groups, except by Karl Menninger, me, and a few other
faculty members. I share this observation without hedging, in
the knowledge that it is entirely typical and probably even
more prevalent in other psychiatric centers. Moreover, I have
learned that ministers would be hard put to know what to
teach, from their own discipline, to members of the psychological professions even if they were specifically asked and
salaried to do so so. Indeed, what basic science, attained
skills, or special arts would they select as relevant? To show
that for me these questions are not rhetorical, let me answer
provisionally by suggesting some viable contributions from

the religious disciplines: ethics, home visiting, the art of conversation, and the sensitive use of symbols in systematic thought and liturgical work.

These four suggestions stem from the next observations I was forced to make. In the past decade, psychiatry went through a third revolution, spurred by the regionalization of mental health services and increased emphasis on prevention. Many psychiatric workers became impatient with the hospital, office, or couch. They wanted to be out where the action was, in the public marketplaces, in schools, courts, social agencies, ghettos, poverty areas, housing developments, political action groups, Common Cause chapters, or school boards. Many ministers before them, becoming impatient with pulpit and parish, also had sought opportunities for intervention and melioration in the public arena. Prophetic ministry enticed some mental health workers into a kind of prophetic psychiatry. More pointedly, the traditional prerogative of pastors to initiate contact with anyone and to visit people in their homes, served consciously or unconsciously as a model to be emulated by many mental health workers in fostering their own goals as agents of prevention or change. Elsewhere[5] I have described this special prerogative as the *pastoral right of initiative and access.* I have begged ministers always to be aware of this right as one of their most unique and valuable functional assets. At any rate, many mental health workers today, driven by their own professional needs and goals, are assuming a quasi-pastoral stance and have good reason to envy pastors this unique pastoral right. Psychiatrists and psychologists, long accustomed to patients' coming to them in a clinic or hospital, have had to learn the subtleties of outreach, home visiting, and making conversation with people who are not formally patients. They have had to de-ritualize their sacred fifty-minute hours; they have had to start working on Sundays and Saturdays; they have had to learn the rituals of social groups; and some have even invented secular liturgies of healing with quasi-sacramental overtones. In all these adaptations, one cannot overlook the influence of the preexisting models of church and pastorate, and the community of faith. This observation is an instance of Talcott Parsons' thesis[6] that the secular world models itself at times after the sacred ethos of institutional religion.

Then came the clincher that led directly to my questions about pastoral diagnosis. Recognizing that the parish or congregation is by tradition the natural habitat of most pastors, my institution decided to shift the practicums of its pastoral care and counseling program from hospital to parish settings, despite criticism from the accreditation agency which at that time did not believe that parishes could be training sites. The majority of our pastors in clinical training would not see psychiatric patients already caught up in the health-illness framework of hospital or clinic. Rather, they would make themselves available to problem-laden people in specific congregations who sought help from their pastor, in their own local church, and within the conceptual and operational framework of that church with its denominational theology, polity, and fiscal arrangements. They were supervised by clinically trained pastors and received didactic instruction from pastors, augmented by teaching and consultation from a few psychiatrists, social workers, and psychologists, including myself. All of the latter profoundly believed that pastoral work can be greatly enhanced by psychological knowledge and skill, but that it is *sui generis*. These nontheological professionals assumed that pastors work within a unique framework of concepts, traditions, symbols, and practices not identical with those of the psychological disciplines. After years of involvement in clinical pastoral education in which the major emphasis had proven to be on maximal transfer of knowledge and skill from the psychological to the theological disciplines, the dice were now loaded so as to stimulate authenticity in pastoral work. And the whole question of diagnosing, i.e., how to size up the problem-laden person, became the touchstone of the diversity between the professions. The pointed phrase was, How do pastors diagnose the people who seek their help?

And so some of my colleagues and I began to attend pastoral case conferences. We read pastoral case reports, saw video tape recordings of pastoral counseling processes in some parish settings, heard what the parishioners sought from their pastors, and listened carefully to these pastors' use of language when they described their observations and interventions. To put my observations in a nutshell, these pastors all too often used "our" psychological language, and frequently the worst selection from it—stultified words such as *depression, paranoid, hysterical.* When urged to conceptualize their observations in their own language, using their own theological concepts and symbols, and to conduct their interviews in full awareness of their pastoral office and church setting, they felt greatly at sea. When clients clearly sought pastoral answers to questions of conscience or correct belief, the pastors tended either to ignore these questions or to translate them quickly into psychological or social-interactional subtleties. By and large, they gave an impression analogous to the misbegotten sausage I described earlier—the theological apperceptions in which they had been trained gave way to a psychological ordering system.

The situation is not quite so bleak as described thus far. I grant that most of the pastors brought pastoral warmth, dedication, zest for helping, perceptiveness, and their own religiousness to their work. Some also brought great natural savvy to their task, and could gently put their parishioners at ease. But despite these gifts, they manifested, and sometimes professed, that their basic theological disciplines were of little help to them in ordering their observations and planning their meliorative moves. They did not quite trust their parishioners' occasional use of theological language and their presentations of theological conflicts. Issues of faith were quickly "pulled" into issues of marital role behavior, adolescent protest against parents, or dynamics of transference in the counseling situation. There seemed to be an implicit suspicion of the relevance of theology, both to any client's life and to the method and content of the pastor's counseling process. They also seemed to like psychological language better than theological language, unaware that psychological terminology no less than theological words can be abused as an intellectual defense against human experience.

From the perspective that I espouse, it is a jarring note when any professional person no longer knows what his basic science is, or finds no use for it. Granted that in most professions the applied science and skill aspects tend to take over in daily work and to become a substantive area of concentration. Yet the anchorage points of professional thought and action must remain clear to provide a base of identity and a source of replenishment. Granted, too, that applied sciences and techniques of practice sometimes have a way of conversely influencing the basic sciences from which they emerged. Still there remains in each discipline a foundational kind of knowledge that determines the permissible language games and the distinctions between assumptions, data, and inferences.

I hope, then, that it has become clear that no political ax-grinding or professional prickliness lurks behind my raising the question of pastoral diagnosis. Clinical pastoral education has come of age, and reached the time to be thinking of its roots. Clinical pastoral work is so widespread and so obviously relevant to the needs of people that its practitioners must now begin to think of its authenticity rather than its propagation. I feel that pluralism in the helping professions has been so zestfully promoted, and is now so well established, that the time has come for some consideration of each profession's specificity and distinctiveness. I think the question of diagnosis is a salient starting point for tackling these issues. I hope it is a manageable and productive topic.

III

A NEW USE FOR
AN OLD WORD: DIAGNOSIS

Although the words "diagnosis" and "to diagnose" seem to have been all but absorbed by medicine, it will surprise no student of Greek to hear that they are general terms. They are used to mean discerning and discriminating in any field of knowledge, distinguishing one condition from another, and, by derivation, resolving or deciding. *Diagignoskein* ("distinguish") is differentiated on the one hand from *dokein* ("seem good," "think"), which leads to opinions and eventually dogmas, and on the other hand from *aisthanesthai* ("apprehend by the senses"), which means to perceive or view close to the level of appearance. To diagnose means grasping things as they really are, so as to do the right thing. Hence, in medicine, diagnosis at its best entails etiology, for the penetrating view arrives at causes and deals with patterns of cause-and-effect relations in the course of illness.

Obviously, these meanings of diagnosis and diagnosing are applicable to a variety of disciplines, including jurisprudence, ethics, sociology, economics and, pointedly, to all the so-called helping professions. One might say that whenever we are presented with a condition, especially one that entails stress, suffering, or unhappiness, which in turn elicits a desire for relief or melioration, the first thing to do is to diagnose that condition. Any would-be helper must know what he is dealing with, otherwise his moves are only shots in the dark. Thus regarded, diagnosis is very much a pastoral task also. It should be a substantial part of any pastor's daily activities. Who would deny that pastors need to approach their charges with a discerning knowledge of their condition, their situation, or their plight, and with discriminate ideas about desirable aid or interventions?

Historically, diagnosis is indeed not foreign to the theological domain. There are at least two great landmarks of theological-diagnostic literature, very different from each other to be sure. Both abound in fine descriptions of, and subtle differentiations between, various conditions, going well beyond surface impressions to grapple with "things as they really are." The first landmark is the *Malleus Maleficarum*[7] of 1480, written by two Dominicans with the explicit intention of providing a diagnostic manual for practicing exorcists. Its focus is on the phenomena of possession and how to distinguish these from other conditions, some of which might be medical. Steeped as it is in demonology, its proximate goal can hardly be called pastoral by present-day standards, or by ancient standards for that matter, unless the burning of bodies at autos-da-fé and the premature sending of souls to their eternal home be considered pastoral activities. Yet its ultimate goal was pastoral, namely, the purification of the soul. The book was written clearly to foster the art of clerical diagnosing. And if we are horrified by this early misdirected endeavor, we have cause to be thankful to the medical profession, which, through the efforts of such men as Johannes Weyer, did its best to come up with more humane alternatives by developing a different diagnostic system altogether. It is a pity, however, that this humanization led in effect to a shift from theological to medical thinking, which siphoned off some legitimate diagnostic functions from theology.

The second landmark is Jonathan Edwards' *A Treatise Concerning Religious Affections*[8] of 1746. It too was written in an era of upheaval and addressed itself to phenomena of religious turmoil. The Great Awakening produced troublesome manifestations which required theological discernment, careful psychological analysis, and eventually some pastoral sorting out of religious sheep from religious goats, so to speak, to foster the cure of souls. Edwards dwelled on the "signs of gracious affections," introducing both positive and negative signs. He spoke of "distinguishing marks" of saintliness and the "qualifications of those that are in favor with God and entitled to his eternal rewards." He was a penetrating diagnostician who went well beyond surface impressions. He distinguished between good and poor diagnostic indicators and felt that some "signs" are suspect, if not worthless. For instance, he saw no diagnostic value in the mere intensity of affections; he would not take body effects and verbosity as yardsticks of conversion. He distrusted some clients' lavish use of Biblical proof texts, and saw no diagnostic value in the mere frequency of worship attendance and profuse engagement in God-talk. By our standards, Edwards' *Treatise* lacks a direct empirical footing; it hinges more on his doctrinal convictions than on observations of living people from his own orbit. To that extent it will strike us today more as a psychologically informed doctrinal study than a pastoral-theological work. It contains no concrete case studies or even vignettes, and does not eventuate in recommendations for specific interventions. What "living documents" or specific persons Edwards refers to are Biblical personalities and a few saints of the church, both remote. Yet his thinking is undoubtedly diagnostic and specifically attuned to the concrete religious situation of his time.

The *Malleus Maleficarum* is a ponderous and highly authoritarian text. Politicized as it was, the diagnostic process became a priestly act imposed on a potential, and likely, victim. It led to a verdict, followed by acts of vengeance or cruelty. Priestly diagnosis in this case was an act of power. Not so in Edwards' *Treatise*. Although the approach is still quite authoritarian, or at least paternalistic, the party being diagnosed takes a hand in arriving at the diagnostic formulation. In fact, Edwards mentions self-examination, which, if it is expressly pursued, implies a process of self-scrutiny and discovery aided by some expert. Parenthetically, how many doctors today have shed the paternalistic heritage to the extent that they would allow the diagnostic process to be a truly participatory enterprise on the part of the patient?

Self-diagnosis of a theological kind was pointedly pursued a century after Edwards by Søren Kierkegaard. His written works[9] give us glimpses of an assiduous diagnostic process, at times bordering on obsessional thought. It is all the more interesting in that the trained theologian and his charge are in this case one and the same person. He artfully conducts an intrapsychic dialogue concealed by introducing two fictitious parties arguing with each other. Kierkegaard does not introduce a diagnostic system, and there is little in his writings that will strike us as pastoral. Nevertheless, his work contains much that can be seen as a demonstration of self-diagnosing within an exquisitely theological framework. There can be no doubt that theology was Kierkegaard's basic science, albeit he never became a practicing minister, let alone a pastor to others. Discerning knowledge was his goal, starting with self-knowledge for the sake of bringing about a desirable change of heart.

This background, then, should be enough to indicate that diagnosis is not a function alien to the theological perspective.

Why, then, is diagnosing so infrequently done in modern pastoral work? Why is it not taught in seminaries—except in Roman Catholic ones, in a fashion, under the rubric of "moral theology"? Why is so little being written about it today in either Protestant or Roman Catholic circles? Could it be that the practice, and even the very notion, of pastoral diagnosing have been discredited by poor applications or by diagnostic systems that misfired?

The answer to the last question is a qualified yes, which also provides a partial answer to the first questions. Condensing complicated chapters of history in a few phrases, it must be said that two leading factors contributed to the demise of diagnosis as a common pastoral activity. One factor was the nature and the basis of the judgments in which the diagnostic process was to eventuate. From the Middle Ages until quite recently Roman Catholic priests arrived at judgments of disposition and behavior that were overweeningly moral judgments. Their pastoral work was guided by canons developed in a special branch of theology called moral theology, the application of which to individual cases was caught up in casuistry. Behind moral theology stood systematic theology and tradition, both of which furnished religious principles for the moral doctrines. Pastoral-theological concern with problems of human living was focused on the rightness or wrongness of motives and acts, amounting at times more to adjudication procedures than to gracious assessments of predicaments from which constructive interventions could be derived. Well after the Reformation, when Protestant pastors wished to divest themselves of this heritage of casuistry, they still found the dice loaded with another traditional factor from which they could not so easily take distance.

That second factor, in a sense more powerful and enduring than the first one, consisted of the pastoral-diagnostician's limited focus, which is captured in the phrase "examination of conscience." What pastors investigated and what parishioners offered for inspection was conscience—no more and no less. To a large extent and for a very long time, the contract between pastors and parishioners remained anchored in the age-old tradition of the penitentials, in which the two parties had to play sharply circumscribed roles. The parishioner's lot was to be a prospective or actual penitent; the priest's role was to hear the confession and pronounce judgment, including the imposition of penances and the pronouncement of divine forgiveness. Just as the patient offered his body and its secretions to the doctor for inspection, the parishioner offered his conscience and its workings to the priest for examination. The mutual roles in the parishioner-priest contract were clear-cut and highly standardized, if not ritualized. Even the anti-casuistical Protestant pastors and parishioners felt tied to them for centuries after the Reformation. One went to his pastor to have his conscience examined, or to be engaged with his pastor in self-examination of his conscience. Other psychological factors, if envisaged at all, were relegated to the background. Let me add that examinations of conscience are not by any means to be decried or belittled. I am making merely the historical point that this traditional emphasis kept pastoral evaluations for a long time in a groove—some will say a rut—from which they could not readily be extricated.

The qualification that now has to be added to our picture of the gradual demise of pastoral diagnosis calls attention to another pastoral tradition. It is the tradition of spiritual

direction. Though often paired with the office of the
confessor and thus liable to the same moralistic encrustations,
the office of spiritual directing had higher aims than sorting
out sins and examining consciences. It could, at its best, take
hold of all of consciousness and even those dark recesses of
the mind which we call the unconscious today, in an effort to
aid the development of a full Christian life suffused with
religious experience that would affect all a person's acts,
thoughts, will, inclinations, and feelings.

One difficulty with this pastoral office, and the investigations it engendered, was its tendency to be authoritarian.
Some pastors directed too hard and barely listened to their
charges. As Michelet pointed out, too many priests seemed
too fond of directing women in particular, in blatantly
paternalistic ways. For Protestants, the word "director" is too
powerful and smacks too quickly of control. But Protestant
and Roman Catholic pastors alike have cherished the role of
adviser to people, examining with them some important
issues in their lives and giving them advice, particularly in
crisis situations. Untold spiritual letters of advice have been
written by pastors, to unknown parishioners as well as to
famous heads of state. Spiritual direction could include
giving solace in bereavement, helping a person sort out the
pros and cons of a career choice, assisting a parishioner
through a crisis of illness, disaster, or war. Needless to say,
the skillful spiritual director needed to make some assessment
of the problems brought to his attention before he could
decide on the proper intervention.

Yet this tradition too is poor in systematic diagnostic
thought. Most of the manuals for spiritual directors are
strong on prescriptions and weak on assessment. They
breathe a therapeutic furor, sometimes to the point of
overreadiness to regulate all human lives into minutiae, with

little regard for individual differences and hardly any recognition of developmental timetables.

If one looks at the current pastoral-theological literature, one finds that not only the word but the very idea of diagnosis seems to be repudiated in pastoral care. Sometime ago I surveyed systematically a number of currently outstanding books on pastoral care and counseling, looking for evidence of a genuinely pastoral-theological diagnostic awareness in ministers. I reported my findings elsewhere:[10] the word "diagnosis" rarely occurs in an index of any of these books, and if it appears at all, it proves to refer to psychiatric or medical usage. (The work of E. Draper is only a seeming exception: the author is a physician and is interested in medical, not pastoral, diagnosis.)[11] One instance of pastoral-diagnostic thought is illustrated by Hiltner[12] in his citation of the work of the nineteenth-century Ichabod Spencer. Hiltner reports that this minister, otherwise quite gifted and astute, seems to have approached one case of pastoral care with the wrong diagnosis, going wildly astray in his efforts to help a distraught woman.

In a much earlier work, Hiltner made at least the effort to seek an approach to the difficult issue of "spiritual diagnosis" (the quotation marks are his) by suggesting that such a diagnosis has three elements: personality diagnosis, situational diagnosis, and spiritual resources diagnosis. The latter element, however, is more an assessment of positive religious values that could be put to therapeutic use by a religious worker than a clear-cut evaluation of the person's spirituality per se, which is likely to have liabilities as well as assets.

The same observation about paucity of pastoral-diagnostic thought is pressed upon the reader of McNeill's thorough text of 1951, *A History of the Cure of Souls*.[13] It shows that the history of pastoral care and counseling has been preoccu-

pied by a poimenic activism that zealously gives counsel or
spiritual guidance, that eagerly corrects, consoles, and does
other things describable as "binding" or "loosing." This
activity may be grafted on great wisdom and consummate
skill in pastoral interventions, but it is devoid of systematic
presentations of diagnostic knowledge to guide the interventions. The pastoral care through the ages recorded in
McNeill's book is driven by zeal, warmth, art, or wisdom,
amounting at times to a *furor therapeuticus*. His curers of
souls are often gifted in intuitive skills of discernment and
endowed in its *art*, but they do not seem to have any desire
for an orderly diagnostic *science* for their interventions.
What few systematic differentiations they acknowledge are
almost entirely of a situational character. The sick, the
bereft, the imprisoned, the dying, and the poor are the
"classes" that shape up in their work, sometimes giving rise to
handbooks for pastoral prayers or sermonettes in these
specific situations. This categorical-situational approach remains valid even in those pastoral traditions which emphasize
private care and counseling as distinct from the corporate and
congregational form of caring prevalent in other denomina-
tions or faith groups.

Seen from this historical angle, the modern clinical pastoral training movement was grafted ambiguously on the
corporate as well as the private care tradition. Its founder,
Anton Boisen,[14] stressed the corporate tradition by approaching his hospital patients as a special congregation, to be
engaged in worship, mutual encouragement, and wholesome
recreation. He wrote a special hymnbook for use in psychiatric hospitals.[15] Most of his followers, however, modeled their
approach on the exquisitely private care of psychotherapy
and secular counseling, which led to the modern forms of
pastoral counseling. Today, after many years of practice and
formalization amounting to an establishment of proven

value, two critical annotations must be made about the role of diagnosis in modern pastoral care and counseling practice.

The first is that clinically trained pastors, if they think diagnostically at all, typically do so by using psychiatric categories and psychiatric language. As pastors, they apply vicariously psychiatric distinctions to their clients. I am saying this without proprietary claims and without implication of thievery. After all, some knowledge about a person's psychological condition should be important to any would-be helper. If such knowledge is freely available from other friends in the helping professions, so much the better. But would not a pastor want to have some knowledge about the person stemming from theological or religious ordering principles? Would he not like to know beforehand, prior to unleashing his therapeutic furor, something about the person's religious situation—his state of grace, his despair, his deep or shaken loyalty, his tenets or disbeliefs, his grounds for hope, if any, his rebelliousness or his tendency to deny any responsibility for himself by the pious sheep talk of the Twenty-third Psalm? These are just a few possibilities which must affect the pastor's choice of interventions, if they are thought to have any relevance at all.

The second note is more technical, stemming from certain reflections about secular counseling techniques which I think are misguided. To put it broadly, the dominant influence on clinical pastoral counseling has for several decades come from the school of Carl Rogers, though this is now waning.[16] This school explicitly scorns any division, in time or principle, between diagnosis and treatment, and goes on to find prior assessment and diagnosis distasteful, for various reasons. At its best, it holds that the counseling process is designed to let the counselee discover for himself what his problems are, with the clarifying help of the counselor, who also seeks to thwart facile or defensive verbalisms and elicit feelings. At its best,

also, this emphasis is meant to honor the client's self-respect
and stimulate his capacity for self-determination. But in
letting things hinge on reportable and expressible feelings,
such an approach tends to restrict itself to conscious phenomena, and to make light of those powerful historical
determinants which have become the client's relatively enduring personality structures. The Rogerians' sharp focus on the
here and now, and on the reportable contents of consciousness, makes the client's problems a priori transitional. It gives
the self a rather ephemeral status, despite the central place
given to it in theory. At its worst, Rogerian theory and
practice find diagnosis offensive, originally because of an
alleged authoritarianism that it found inherent in all diagnosing, then because of unnecessary laboriousness, and lately
because it is seen as anti-humanistic.

There is far more to any person than what he thinks
himself to be, which should be no revelation to those who
hold a lapsarian view of man. In that view, anyone's
self-regard and self-knowledge are beset by all manner of
demonic deceptions. As to the Rogerian objections to
diagnosis, more needs to be said. Granted that some
diagnosticians, in medicine and psychiatry, do proceed in
authoritarian ways, that is their personal fault and does not
follow from the idea of diagnosing. Granted too that some
theological diagnoses in the past have amounted to authoritarian dispositions over the very lives of men, this aberration
does not invalidate the idea of making theological judgments
in the pastoral assessment of anyone's condition. Neither
does the fact that some conditions are puzzlesome enough to
require careful study make the diagnostic process laborious,
let alone unnecessarily so. Central to my rebuke of the
alleged anti-humanism in diagnosis, in any professional perspective, is the conviction that people in difficulties have the
right to be taken seriously in their complaints. No stone

should be left unturned in determining the nature of their difficulties before taking remedial steps. Humanism requires thoroughness, with acute perception and reasoning.[17]

Though it is true that thoughtful therapeutic work is a process that refines, and sometimes alters, the original diagnosis so that one could say "therapy is diagnosis," there are also grounds for reversing this proposition. "Diagnosis is therapy" holds that evaluation often has by itself some healing effect, if only in making the client's or patient's problem more tangible by giving it a focus. The processes of diagnosis and therapy undoubtedly shade into each other, but that does not mean that one can dispense with either.

Thus it is that most practicing pastors today, including those with clinical pastoral training, have an anti-diagnostic bent. And those using vicariously any system of psychiatric diagnosis for a foothold seem thereby to imply that diagnosing ipso facto is not a theological or pastoral activity, but a medical prerogative.

In the meantime, one important professional question keeps cropping up that is doomed to remain unanswered as long as the pastors' diagnostic nihilism prevails. In multidisciplinary settings under psychiatric auspices, in which clinically trained chaplains are full participants in various phases of work with patients, it is often asked in what way the pastor's work is different from anyone else's on the team. Such explicitly religious activities as worship leadership, administering Sacraments, convening religious study groups, or acting as liaison agent between the institution and the patient's home church are clearly his responsibility. But what special basic or applied science or art does the chaplain bring to bear on the diagnostic and therapeutic processes in such institutions? In my experience and in the light of published studies on this question,[18] chaplains are vulnerable to anyone's interpretation of their role. The most whimsical opinions for or against their usefulness in these settings prevail because they themselves seem to dodge the issues. Most of them cannot answer the question decisively in clear conceptual terms. They seem content to let the answer rest on attitudes of goodwill on the part of the rest of the staff or, strangely enough, on being appreciated as able but nondescript therapists whose personal assets lift them luckily above their professional background. Without in the least questioning the role of clinically trained chaplains in psychiatric hospitals, and the several specific functions for which they need to be pastors and theologians, I am now focusing on those less-circumscribed functions which other team members would call "psychiatric," namely, in diagnosis, treatment, or prevention.

This question of the pastor's specific competence is not nearly so acute in medical clinics or hospitals, but for the wrong reasons. The parlance and ingrained habits of those places allow for an easy distinction between body and mind (or that nebulous entity "spirit") which has for centuries guided a practical division of labor between the main parties. "Where the doctor leaves off or has to admit his failure, the priest's or minister's work begins." I do not condone this phrase; I only point out that its rationale is entrenched. Untold numbers of books have been written about mind, body, soul, and spirit that keep such facile territorial divisions intact, with neat picket fences around everyone's acre. Even the clients are talked into recognizing and maintaining these boundaries. The attitude is, "Of course the pastor does not diagnose or give treatment in such places, for diagnosis pertains only to those 'parts' or 'aspects' of the patient to which medicine has access. Whatever the minister does pertains to the patient's other dimensions."

But what are those extra-medical and extra-psychiatric dimensions? In what special perspective can they be grasped?

What kinds of words are germane to this perspective? What kinds of people are responsible for earmarking, describing, and conceptualizing it? To answer these questions, we must turn to the clients. To put my position on this in a nutshell: I believe that problem-laden persons who seek help from a pastor do so for very deep reasons—from the desire to look at themselves in a theological perspective.

IV

WHY DO PEOPLE
TURN TO PASTORS?

In the previous pages, our focus was on the pastor's professional specificity in the context of theoretical diversity. We have noted the practical interactions between the theological and psychological disciplines. The person to be helped, the client, the patient, the problem-laden soul, remained a remote third party receiving only indirect references. We must now pay our full attention to him.

Why do problem-laden people in such large numbers turn to their pastors first in seeking help? The answers that have been given to this question are quite diverse. In rural areas, pastors are often the only accessible source of help. Here they are forced to play many roles that are parceled out differently in urban areas. Where scarcity of resources is not the main problem, economic considerations have been advanced in answer to our question. Pastors, and the churches in which they operate, tend to render personal services free or at low cost, at least in the initial stages of a person's help-seeking endeavors. Moreover, in areas where other services are available, pastors are trusted as referral channels and triage agents whose advice is appreciated when the question is, "Where can I get help?" Precisely in that capacity pastors are seen by other professionals, rightly or wrongly, as first-line mental health workers, first-line legal advisers, first-line social workers—first-line counselors and caretakers in many different respects. They are sometimes house finders for the homeless and people on the move, and are in that sense first-line real estate brokers.

There is so much face validity in these answers that one would hardly dare press for deeper reasons. Yet on closer inspection the typical answers all give short shrift to the client. They reduce his motives for turning to his pastor to some set of situational variables. They suggest that the client feels caught in some way and has practically no recourse other than trying out his pastor for advice. Because of their plausibility, these answers eliminate at once any more deep-seated preference a help-seeking person may have for a pastor. One could argue, however, that the pastoral triage situation which I have described already implies some freedom of choice for the help-seeking person. If other resources are locally available, if they are known, and if economic factors play no crucial role, why would some persons still seek pastoral advice first, even for referral? Is it not likely that they trust his judgment, his know-how, his confidentiality, or his assumed frame of reference more than somebody else's? By virtue of their choice of first seeking pastoral help, are they not asking for their problems to be placed in a pastoral perspective? In seeking a pastoral answer, even if recognizing that his may be only a first or tentative answer, are they not placing themselves voluntarily into a value system, and into an ambiance of special tradition and communion which they consider relevant?

My answer to these questions is an unhesitating yes! Granted that every pastor knows of perfunctory help-seeking behavior by parishioners, and that under the pressure of schedules his own initial response may occasionally turn out to be perfunctory. People with problems usually know that there are many sides to their predicaments, allowing their condition to be placed in different perspectives. In turning to a pastor they give a signal—they want his perspective, and they want it first. They want it most urgently, or they would not have bothered to come. They present themselves perhaps bunglingly, for they are under some kind of stress. But they may want to confess, to open up, to lay bare a secret, to share an anguish, to be consoled, to be rescued from despair, to be taken to task, to be held responsible, to be corrected for attitudes they suspect are wrong, or to be restrained in their intentions. They may want to be blessed, encouraged, admonished, or even rebuked. The mind of man is complex, and the heart infinitely more so. One can count on it that some self-evaluation has already been attempted before the person turns to his pastor, just as he is likely to have taken some aspirin before going to his doctor. The motives and moves of help-seeking persons should never be sold short.

So let us try our question again, this time barring expeditious reasons as answers. Why do problem-laden people in such large numbers turn to their pastors first in seeking help? One person says in a phone call to his pastor: "Yes, I know there are psychiatrists in this town, and a family service center, and several social agencies. They say there is also a very good marriage counseling center. In fact, my son goes there right now. But I want to talk things over with you first." Here is an unwavering search for pastoral help, a purposive selectivity on the client's own initiative. Several reasons have been advanced for this action.[19]

One reason is that some persons who are religious particularists or sectarians approach their priest or minister to explore with him where they can turn safely for help from some specialist within their faith group, denomination, or sect if possible, or beyond these if it must be. They turn their pastor into a referral agent for reasons they explicitly connect with their faith. From conviction or fear, they seek safety—some guarantee that Dr. So-and-So is respectful of their religion and understanding of its demands or rituals, and will not tinker with their faith or values.

Even I as a psychologist have been approached in this manner by prospective patients, some going so far as to claim my special attention, asking priority for themselves because of denominational identity. I find this penchant itself a fascinating diagnostic problem. Habitually I turn such a claim into a brief crisis intervention that deals with the patient's present inability to make flexible use of his community's resources, or, as the case may be, with the grandiosity or magical expectations embedded in this request. Why would he restrict himself to a denominational matching game? What is he so scared of? Is he really ready for treatment? Does he think he is so special? These are all questions raised by one psychologist who is alert to the uses and misuses of religion, and who is not a fierce particularist in religion. Some of his colleagues will promptly allow themselves to be matched by the prospective patient on denominational grounds alone, perhaps making the most of it by acting on their own sectarian penchants, turning their helping endeavors into a therapeutic *entre nous* between like-minded believers.

While pastors may wish to respond to such approaches in different ways, the point I want to make is that such clients seek, among other things, religious counsel. Their beliefs drive them into the study of their pastor. They want their problems sized up and tackled within a definite frame of reference. They want their tradition to speak to them, they want to discuss themselves in familiar terms; they want a glimpse of the light of their faith to clarify their predicament. Whatever else they may wish from their pastor or church, they want some denominational channeling of their problem-solving efforts including, if need be, the church's permission to temporarily step out of its channel. Though the person may have a poor understanding of his faith and formulate his inquiry awkwardly, he raises a theological question and knocks for this purpose at the right door. How disappointing, then, when his pastor quickly translates his quest into psychological or social terms, and fails to give him a theological answer! Or when he forgoes the opportunity for some religious re-education, from which the client may learn to raise better theological questions!

Another answer to our question is that many persons do not really know what they seek from their pastor in turning to him for help. They consider him a good all-round caretaker whose own alleged faith or evangelical zeal will induce him to make precious time available to a sincere soul. One comes with a drinking problem; another one has just beaten his wife and now feels ashamed; a third one has long lived in marital discord and now contemplates a divorce. And so a counseling process starts, focused on addiction, aggression, or separation. Feelings are brought out, clarification is given, the client's stronger or better self is appealed to, and some light becomes visible at the end of the tunnel. Depending on the pastor's style and persuasion, there may have been a lively therapeutic interaction with much active support from the counselor, or there may have been a patient scrutiny of the client's repeated attitudes toward his helper. Perhaps there was an intentional use of transference phenomena and an assiduous analysis of their origins. If the latter occurred, the pastor would come to know something of the conscious and unconscious reasons why the parishioner sought him out for help. Maybe he had some theological grounds for making contact with a pastor and seeking church auspices for his problem-solving attempts. Maybe he knew dimly that coming to terms with his father was something like coming to terms with God. Perhaps he believed that feelings of guilt have an aspect of sinfulness.

It may also happen, however, that the pastor's counseling technique keeps the focus on marital interaction or the problem drinker's low self-esteem and inability to express anger in forthright terms, without the slightest allusion to any theology of wife-beating, self-loathing, and feelings of wrath. One may balk at first at this odd-sounding sentence: we used to think that drinking was sinful but have just learned that it is an illness, and we believe that wife-beating is an aberration of impulse control, or some kind of sadism.

My point is that what any of these things "is" depends on the framework in which it is taken up, on the light in which it is regarded, on the perspective in which it comes to the fore. Nothing *is* anything in particular unless it appears in a framework which gives it a name, describes it, and starts a series of mental operations upon it. To do this is the task of any discipline, the prerogative of any science or art. A pastor is ipso facto a theologian, who has the right, nay, the duty, to put anything he wants in a theological perspective. He may use other perspectives besides, if helpful in his profession, or if he has a broad curiosity. But wife-beating is no less theological than it is psychological or sociological or criminological. It may be endocrinological for all we know. What it "is" depends on how it is regarded.

Now what bearing do these theoretical considerations have on the person with a problem seeking help from his pastor? My answer arises from cases of clinical pastoral candidates which I have supervised, or to whom I have been a consultant, as well as from a general awareness of the complexity of human problems. I am convinced that a great many persons who turn to their pastor for help in solving personal problems seek assistance in some kind of religious or moral self-evaluation. They want to see some criteria of their

faith applied to themselves. They may not be able to say so
outright, for fear of giving the impression of piosity. They
may remain silent about their longing for a religious evaluation after discovering that their pastor seems to be on a
different wavelength. They may not know how to phrase
their wish, hoping that their pastor will make the first move in
that direction by offering the right words or making the
pertinent allusions. Some may simply wish to pray, if only
the pastor would offer to do so. Some may wish to be blessed,
if only their pastor would be so inclined. Others may wish to
be decisively confronted with their failings or disloyalties, if
only their pastor had the forthrightness to do so. What
parishioners expect from their pastor emerges from a complicated mixture of hopes, fears, fantasies, ambivalent feelings,
and reality testing, all charged with a double set of numinous
values: on the one hand those inherent in religion and the
transcendent, on the other hand the numinosity of parental
power and grandeur experienced in early childhood. Pastors
are transference figures par excellence, not necessarily by
what they are as persons but by the projections of those who
seek their counsel.

I think these considerations have an important bearing on
referral. If a pastor thinks of himself as a gatekeeper to the
helping resources of his community and thus engages in much
referral work, he should try to discern whether the help-
seeking person really wanted him to be a gatekeeper only.
Did the client seek a conjoint pattern of help for himself:
pastoral counsel or care in addition to the medical, legal, or
psychiatric care to which he has now been referred? In either
case, the grounds for referral need scrutiny. Particularly in
referrals to psychiatrists, pastors often use the *seriousness* of
the client's disturbance as criterion for referral. This in turn
gives a quasi-quantitative character to the distinction between "counselee" and "patient," as it has done in the past to

the distinction between "counseling" and "therapy." In this conception of practice, pastors deal with "mild" or "moderate" conditions, leaving the "severe" conditions to the psychological disciplines to handle.

While this may be an expeditious division of labor, it is based on inconsistent thinking. The distinctions here used between mild and severe are psychological, not theological. In applying them, the pastor makes a vicarious psychiatric judgment, a tentative psychiatric diagnosis in rough outline. He also implicitly assumes that a person cannot be a counselee and a patient at once, that he cannot be engaged at the same time in a pastoral and a psychiatric helping relationship. The person is thus forced to regard himself in one perspective at a time, instead of in a multiperspectival view. This may be sound in some cases, but should not be enthroned as dogma.

I would emphasize again that pain and suffering are always complex and multidimensional experiences, often crying out for enlightenment and resolution in several perspectives at once. Equally important for our concern with pastoral diagnosis is the fact that the pastoral referral to another profession is likely to proceed from a peculiar tacit assumption, namely, that theological ideas become inoperative in the face of serious mental turmoil. This in turn fosters the myth that the healthy and the sick are two entirely different species of man. If we have learned anything from psychiatry, we should stress, rather, the prevailing dynamic continuities that exist between man and man, and the essential sameness of everyone's unconscious.

In the meantime, our poor client may have been effectively thwarted from his original intention to apply a theological perspective to himself with the help of a pastoral expert. While he may find that his pastor has been helpful to him in referring him to another profession from which real

benefits may be gained, he may also feel disappointed in his
pastor. In effect the pastor slighted the serious religious
soul-searching that the person had hoped to accomplish with
his help. The pastor sold a secular product where the
parishioner had hoped to obtain a sacred one. The latter is
puzzled. Why did not his pastor come through with the
symbols of his faith? Why did he not attempt a pastoral, i.e.,
theological diagnosis? Why was he, the help-seeking person,
not taken seriously enough to be thoroughly evaluated in his
soul's anguish, within the perspective he took for granted
when turning to his pastor?

We should now follow the problem-laden person to his
next possible situation. He has become a patient—indeed, he
is in a psychiatric hospital. It is a good place by any standard:
with a high staff-patient ratio, this hospital's treatment is
indeed individualized; the staff is thoroughly interdisciplinary
and dedicated to teamwork. The spirit is at once humane
and scientific. The patients themselves take an active hand in
governing their milieu. The hospital has a competent,
well-trained chaplain who loves his work and is respected by
staff and patients alike. In this setting, the patient may again
seek pastoral help, and so he turns to the chaplain.

What will they talk about and in what perspective will
they proceed with each other? Chances are that the chaplain
already knows much about the patient's "basic conflicts," for
he participates regularly in case conferences. He also has had
one or more private interviews with the patient, and has
shared his impressions with the diagnostic team. He too
found the patient "depressed," or "extremely suspicious."
Shrewd clinician that he is, he even noticed that the patient,
under the influence of his pious but overbearing mother, and
his weak, uncommunicative father who was himself a minister's son, felt uncomfortable in his presence because he finds
all religious believers hypocrites. Yes, it might be better to

focus all the patient's talk and attitudes and activities on his relations to motherly figures.

This is, of course, a fictitious situation, but I think its essential features are rather common. The chaplain merges as it were with the psychiatric team of which he is a member. His observations are added to the observations of other specialists and they are all rounded off into an evaluative narrative from which a diagnostic summary emerges. All kinds of persons have contributed to that narrative—social workers, nurses, internists, chaplains, and others. But the eventual summary is psychiatric in its concepts, language use, and point of view. And that is defensible, for this is a psychiatric hospital. Luckily, psychiatry is a broad, holistic perspective which encompasses many data. Meanwhile, the non-psychiatrists on the team have engaged in greater or lesser accommodations of their own points of view to the psychiatric perspective. Some have made no accommodations at all—the internist almost defiantly has used his own language and the esoteric symbols of his laboratory reports. Luckily, the psychologist's viewpoint and language are so close to psychiatry that they hardly present a problem. The social worker, however, who interviewed the family, reports his observations to a large extent in psychiatric terms and may have conducted the interviews in the same manner. There is precious little of sociology in his findings, except for some phrases about income levels and social class. The nurse, bless her, is always down to earth and speaks plain English. The chaplain's contribution is a feat of accommodation. Even when he might have focused on the patient's church relations or engagements in ritual, much as the social worker might have focused on his family or job relations, he took only "his" slice of the patient's life, but examined it in psychiatric fashion. In this interdisciplinary assessment, the patient was carved up into bits of behavior, or he was regarded as an actor in different situations, each expert dealing with a special piece or situation. This is essentially a spatial approach, in which the disciplines do not come into their own or work with reciprocity.

I am exposing these professional manners almost sadly, certainly without glee. One aim is to show the strength of the drift toward accommodation. Another is to demonstrate that this drift is unevenly distributed among the cooperating professions, and that some disciplines come close to losing their specificity. Some professions remain closer to their basic science than others, for whatever reason. But my main goal is to show that even in situations of the utmost goodwill and the greatest competence, all is not well with the identity of pastors and with the relations between the theological and psychological disciplines.

We are now looking at this problem from the patient's point of view. What chance does the patient have, if he so desires, to take a good theological look at himself with the help of an expert trained in that way of looking? In one study of the role of the chaplain in a psychiatric hospital a patient expressed the wish that the chaplain might participate in group leisure-time activities, meaning "bull sessions" in which religious questions could be discussed. Others wanted him to make "friendly floor visits," "be a friend," "be an understanding individual," and "to pray for us." [20]

Who can sort out in the last statement sarcasm from deep wish? And who would denigrate the longing for just "a friend" when we know that thousands of people find numinous depth in an obese, inarticulate, and affluent adolescent from India, revered beyond any demonstrated merit? There is reason to think that some pastors really do not know what people are looking for in seeking their help. Because pastors keep their own theological viewpoint submerged, or do not know what to do with it in a personal situation, they thwart the client's efforts to use the theological approach to problems forthrightly.

There are, however, some hopeful signs. Some hospital chaplains are trying to interview the patients in order to discover their religious or moral values and come to know their deepest beliefs. Having learned some lessons from the past, they do not proceed with checklists of virtues and vices, they do not rub in sin, and they do not preach sermonettes during their interviews. Moreover, they do not impose bans and do not assign specific acts of penance. They could, of course, if they wished and felt strongly about these things. In fact, I know of a psychiatric hospital case in which the patient insisted that a ritual foot washing be administered to him by the brethren of his communion.[21] After the hospital chaplain had overcome staff resistance to this odd demand and had made arrangements for this rite, the whole staff agreed that this event had proved to be a turning point in the patient's course from illness to health.

But the pastors and chaplains who do want to project their theology into their pastoral work, and who wish to be clear about their professional identity, have a hard time finding appropriate theological categories for approaching their patients and responding to their needs. This difficulty is particularly prominent in regard to diagnosis, i.e., in making discerning pastoral-theological evaluations of the person's problems. By comparison, it seems easier to engage directly in pastoral acts, deeds, or rituals. These have become sufficiently stylized to engender the feeling in the pastor that when he engages in them, he is really doing something meaningful and worthwhile. Not so with pastoral diagnosis. It has very little articulate precedent in the literature; seminaries do not teach it, and the few historical examples on record are in disrepute.

There is still another angle on the expectations of troubled persons who are turning to their pastors for help. The clientele of the various helping professions are beginning to claim rights: the right to adequate services, the right to receive medical treatment, the right to be hospitalized without curtailment of civil rights, the right of access to diagnostic and treatment records, etc. For our purposes, the important theme running through these various claims is that the troubled person, in whatever context he is seeking help, feels he has a right to be taken seriously.

If he seeks help in a medical context, he assumes the role of patient. He fully expects to be diagnosed, and he will demand that the diagnostic investigations be thorough. If at some later time his condition worsens, and if, by hindsight, he has reasons to doubt the thoroughness of the diagnostic work, he may entertain the thought of suing his physician for malpractice. In medicine today, diagnostic work must be painstakingly done, or else the physician risks social and legal assaults on his professional integrity—and his capital! Welfare clients and those seeking assistance from various social agencies have organized to demand their rightful share of moneys and services, with prompt delivery. Whatever they may seek in tangible assistance, theirs is a clear case of wanting in the first place something intangible—the maintenance of their human dignity.

The clue we should take from these social movements and civil rights struggles is that troubled people who seek help from various professions have come to feel that they must be given a dignified, participatory role in teasing out what their troubles are and in deciding what can or should be done to ameliorate their predicament. Authoritarian or paternalistic styles of helping will no longer be tolerated, and many entrenched habits and rituals of the helping professions are placed under scrutiny. All these stirrings have a profound bearing on the question of diagnosis.

For instance, in psychiatry, there are serious misgivings about diagnoses that are little more than attempts to classify a person and tag him with a label taken from some diagnostic manual. Psychiatrists themselves[22] have protested against such diagnoses, notably Karl Menninger. They have offered radically new approaches in which the diagnosis becomes essentially a concise formulation of the person's problem, so worded that leads for therapeutic intervention will logically follow from it. Menninger's *The Vital Balance*,[23] which I have coauthored, also laid the groundwork for the next development in psychiatric diagnosis which in my opinion consists of letting the patient be the central figure in the diagnostic process. What I mean is that, ideally, the patient should be enabled to make a self-diagnosis. Humane care of troubled persons demands the utmost respect for them, which means among other things, that no stone be left unturned in searching out, with them and by their active involvement in a personal relationship to some helper or expert, what the problem is and what might be done about it. The patient has a right to gain the utmost clarity about his condition and to take an active hand in assessing his own predicament. If a person feels caught, he should be given an opportunity to know the snares that trap him.

Put more radically, such revisions of the diagnostic process place the diagnostician, to whatever profession he belongs, in the role of a counselor with special expertise in a particular perspective of knowledge. According to an old designation, attorneys and lawyers are "counselors at law," a title which beautifully describes the kind of role for which I am an advocate. By analogy, physicians could be "counselors in medicine" and pastors could be seen as "counselors in religion, theology, or 'the Christian life.'" I put it this way in order to contrast the diagnostic attitudes I am advocating with some traditional ones which were beset by the tempta-

tion of professionals—judges, doctors, social workers, clergymen, psychiatrists, etc.—to lord it over their fellowmen by
trapping them into their bureaucratic nets. Criticism of old
forms of diagnosis should lead to better forms of diagnosis,
not to the simpleminded negativism of anti-diagnostic posi-
tions.

I believe that the first duty of any professional is to achieve
clarity about the problems brought before him for the sake of
guiding the interventions he is to contemplate. This is a first
duty to his client or patient as well as to his science. If he
does not fulfill this duty, he is a charlatan, albeit perhaps a
very "nice" one—whatever his shield proclaims him to be. Or
he is only a variant of the old-fashioned vendor of patent
medicines standing on his soapbox in the marketplace, selling
his one little vial of liquid as the remedy for "seventy-eight
known diseases."

Diagnosis in any helping profession is the exploratory
process in which the troubled person is given an opportunity
to assess and evaluate himself in a defined perspective, in
which certain observations are made and specific data come
to light, guided by conceptual or operational tools, in a
personal relationship with a resource person. This is prelimi-
nary to decisions about a remedial course of action which the
parties are to take jointly. Each perspective is unique and has
its own integrity, though different perspectives may be placed
on one and the same bit of raw observation or experience.
However we define the psychiatrist's perspective, it is not and
cannot be the same as the dentist's, the sociologist's, the
pastor's. And so, whatever psychiatric diagnosis is, it is not
and cannot by any stretch of goodwill or cooperativeness be
the same as dental, sociological, or pastoral diagnosis. Even
the most outspoken holistic ambitions, which are certainly
present in today's psychiatry and have always been inherent
in theology, cannot make psychiatric and theological diagno-

sis identical. Sharing great breadth of focus does not make two perspectives the same.

Our concern is with the authenticity of pastoral diagnostic work. This is inherent in the multitude of reasons why troubled persons turn to their pastors for help. There was a time when I absolved myself from any obligation toward the pastor's authenticity, arguing that, because I was a psychologist, this was none of my business. I was bold enough, however, to appeal to some pastors to reflect on the issue, and remedy it. Now I feel that I myself may try to make some contribution to it, in a consulting capacity, despite my different professional identity. For I have come to see that in the desired interdisciplinary pooling of resources in the helping professions, the specificity of each discipline is a great asset. Sometimes psychiatry is sold short of the uniqueness of pastoral expertise for which it opted when chaplains became collaborating team members. And conversely, some clients are sold short when they selectively and purposefully turn to their pastor for help, to find that they receive only a bit of psychological advice, however good and solid and opportune that bit of advice may be.

V

GUIDELINES FOR PASTORAL DIAGNOSIS

Maybe I can be of help to pastors by sharing some constructive thoughts about the concepts that may guide the pastoral diagnostic interview. Some of these have been tried out provisionally by a few pastors of local churches and institutional chaplains with whom I have collaborated. I myself have, of course, never conducted a pastoral interview. But I have always been interested in any patient's religious views, belief system, and value orientation[24]—not as isolated data but as factors which qualify his experience and interact with his perceptions and actions. Such information is important for what it allows us to state about his felt personhood and conflicts. My work in the psychology of religion is both an expression of and a stimulus to this diagnostic interest. And since I find science a playful activity, I ask you to let me tinker with a few ideas in the hope that, if you like it, you yourself may play along and eventually produce a better game.

To set the stage realistically, let me say that one of my friends and correspondents, a professor of pastoral theology in a European university, does not like the idea of pastoral diagnosis at all. He objects to my article on this topic by saying: "We—pastors—proclaim the word"; the pastor "tries to view people through the eyes of Christ, as being on the way to the Kingdom, and see how far they are from it"; "we try to portray God's grace and forgiveness through an existential testimony and encounter," and we "embed the person in a community of faith." I find nothing objectionable in this definition of pastoral work, though I think it rather one-sided, but I fail to see anything in it that militates against pastoral assessment, i.e., pastoral diagnosis. In fact, seeing how far anyone is from the Kingdom requires some perspicacity and attentive listening to the client's gropings for self-evaluation. Also proclaiming the word requires some awareness of the audience's capacity to hear; encounter with people presupposes a respectful recognition of another person whose integrity is to be met, and in whose situation or condition one takes a lively interest.

In pondering a set of diagnostic variables for pastoral assessment, I tried to check myself by a few caveats. The ordering principles should not be pointedly and exclusively psychological, medical, psychiatric, or sociological. They should be chosen so as to be readily recognizable to theologians—to systematic, Biblical, historical, practical, and pastoral theologians alike, whatever their subtle differences and historical traditions. They should produce empirical differentiations, both to the helper and the helped. They should be amenable to interview situations. They should span conscious and unconscious levels of organization wherever possible. They should have phenomenological aptness, richness, and diversity to capture personal idiosyncrasies. They should yield a picture of the person, even if only a sketch or telling fragment, from which pastoral strategies for intervention can be developed, for that is the obvious goal and basic justification of all diagnosing.

One of the first dimensions of experience I would wish to assess is the person's *awareness of the Holy*. What, if anything, is sacred to him? What does he revere? Is there anything he regards as untouchable or inscrutable? Does he know what a feeling of reverence is? Admittedly, these terms come straight from Schleiermacher[25] and Otto.[26] They are introduced here for good reasons, for both men were interested in empirical categories and attuned to direct human experiences. They were both phenomenologists of a sort, interested in ascertaining and describing at low levels of abstraction what they felt to be a primary theological datum. And they were interested in the feelings connected with the experience of the Holy, not just in correct thoughts about it. Seeking a primordial stratum of experience, they went right down to the *Ur* quality of these feelings. They had a gift for moving freely between high and low levels of abstraction, which is just what every professional person must do when he goes back and forth between his knowledge base and the concrete situations of his practice.

The pastor would not start by asking his client whether he has read Schleiermacher or knows of Otto, just as the surgeon will not converse with his patient about Lister, but carefully inquires about pain and infections. The pastor, like the psychiatrist, listens with a third ear which in this case may profit from being attuned to Schleiermacher or Otto. Does the person who wants help present himself as a dependent creature, or is he greatly self-inflated and prepossessed with himself? Can he prize something outside himself? If pressed by dire circumstances, for what would he be willing to make any sacrifice?

Has he ever experienced a feeling of awe, or bliss? When, and in what situations? The client may constrict himself to a dry, unemotional factualness that shies away from any mystery and rules out anything transcendent. If so, is that disciplined intellectual positivism pursued with some gusto, or does it seem to be the result of having his fingers burned?

It might be a withdrawal response, saddled with not so disciplined memories of pain. He may consider nothing holy, concealing all feelings by a carefully rehearsed emotional flatness. He may strike the pastor as pedantic, with an air of self-sufficiency while ostensibly asking for help.

The pastor may gently test these impressions. How does a person's sense of creatureliness come through? Sometimes one's willingness to accept the inevitable demonstrates an awareness of his own limits. Sometimes a person indicates his feeling of powerlessness by having an appropriate degree of humility, particularly in the face of omnipresent and besetting human problems, such as pain, suffering, evil, sickness, death, or loss. But what passes for humility may be cockiness or a meddlesome demandingness, particularly in cases of pious humility that insists on preferential treatment by God and demands from him favorable arrangements, especially after the hour of death. Untold private mansions in heaven have been fantasized and enormous deposits of merit have been accumulated by seemingly humble souls who in the end refuse to let God be God. Since Adam, they have always secretly wanted to replace the Creator, but went through the polite formalities he seemed to insist on. They played what they took to be his game.

I am now obviously and freely using theological and even Biblical language in order to make clear what I am driving at. No God-talk is needed in the pastoral diagnostic interview, although there should be no ban on it. What is needed is theological alertness—the tacit guidance the pastor receives from his basic discipline while he deals with a concrete individual who may talk about bereavement or anger or great disappointments.

I think that awareness of the Holy and reverential feelings are also important pastoral diagnostic variables because of their potency to elicit what theologians would call idolatry.

Someone may treat his car so reverently and make so many sacrifices for it in time, money, and energy that other pursuits and objects are bound to suffer from lack of attention. Someone may find the flag so holy or prize his war decoration so much that the Government and the Constitution appear to be his God—a rather clear case of civil religion. Holiness and reverence may be displaced from proper to improper symbols, which is, incidentally, one way of defining idolatry. As diagnosticians, pastors should be immensely curious about the gods of their clients, not taking their God-talk for granted but trying to find out what it refers to in thought and action. If there is any truth in the text "Where your treasure is, there will your heart be also," the exploration of the heart will give a clue to the treasure and vice versa, which is no mean diagnostic lead.

A second diagnostic variable I wish to explore is best designated as *Providence*. It is a straight theological, even a doctrinal, term. The concept can be handled at different levels. The level I want to emphasize for purposes of interviewing is capsuled in a phrase from the psychoanalyst Ernest Jones: "What one really wants to know about the Divine Purpose is its intention *toward oneself*." [27] Abstract doctrinal definitions of Providence are one thing—coming to terms with its personal import is quite another. I think that pastoral interview situations are commonly loaded with implied references to Providence, in just that pinpointed self-reference that Jones had in mind. Troubled persons are understandably upset about the ratio of goodwill and ill will that comes their way, witness that first typical question or exclamation: "Why? Why am I so besieged?" And invariably the next question is: "Why *me*? What have I done to deserve this?" Indeed, what is the "Divine Purpose" in its intention toward myself?

In this personal sense, Providence is a shorthand word for

several crucial types of experience. It may allude to belief in cosmic benevolence. The pastor may ask, "Is there anything good or friendly in your world, or is it all misery?" Or he may comment: "Gosh, that's bleak. . . . I wonder whether you see any light anywhere." Providence may allude to a desire for guidance from somewhere on high, the client muttering, "If I only knew what God's will is." In addition, it refers to a need for nurture: "Tell me, Pastor, where I can find solace. What must I do? What have I left undone? What should I try to change in myself?"

Providence is crucially related to the capacity for trust. Without trust, there is no Providence. Instead, everything is malevolence or threat of harm. Does the person really trust the pastor to whom he has come? Does he trust that the pastor can help him? Does he trust that he himself can be helped at all, and that he is worthy of help? Does he trust that his pastor believes in a larger source of help—a fountain of benevolence with "living water"? Does he know and trust that pastoral care is really divine care mediated? If so, the prognostic outlook is not so bleak. If not, other things must be explored. For there are persons who actively disbelieve in Providence and make no bones about it. They may not know what benevolence is because they have never encountered it. They have had no real experience of it. They do not trust anybody. Objectively, they may have ample reasons for distrusting everybody—parents, clergy, jailers, teachers, church, God, the universe. They have no hope, and know no grounds for hoping. They do not know what it is to be cared for: "My one foster parent who seemed to care during that year in high school died in an accident."

Providence can also be rebuffed from feelings of great personal competence. Cases like this are not prone to seek pastoral help. But since feelings are rarely pure and simple, proud people nevertheless are found in pastors' offices, and often display narcissistic self-sufficiency while asking for help. Maybe they have a dim awareness that their air of self-sufficiency or solipsistic triumph is only an air, a bungled self-presentation behind which lurks the need to be contradicted. Maybe they surmise it is wrong on some grounds, and perhaps they came precisely to receive some judgment.

With the idea of Providence as a beacon, the pastor can make more subtle diagnostic observations that tell him much about where his client is. This beacon is a sure guide to the dynamics of hoping and promising, which are of such therapeutic importance. Following Gabriel Marcel,[28] I feel that hoping and wishing are two entirely different processes. One who hopes is concerned with attitudes and global benefits, such as life, freedom, deliverance, salvation; one who wishes tends to focus on specific things: money, rain after a drought, expensive birthday presents, the death of his enemy. The hoper tests reality, the unbridled wisher engages in magical thought. The hoper refers and defers to a transcendent power that has its own unfathomable purpose; the wisher bends it down to conform to himself. In theological language, the hoper is an eschatologist who lets God be God, the wisher is only an apocalyptist, who seeks reversals of his fate in which his revengeful fantasies will be fulfilled to the letter. The hoper says, "Now I see through a glass darkly . . . ," while the wisher cherishes his room reservation in a heavenly motel.

The other side of hoping and wishing is promising, which I also take to be an aspect of Providence in Jones's sense— namely, how one takes the Divine Purpose in its relation to oneself. Reflections on what any person thinks his God has promised to him throw some light on his character. Does he feel and act as if God owes him specific benefits, including a prompt solution to his present problem, or does he have the humility to feel that God's promised presence is enough, and all he has to go by? And in the same vein, does the person feel that the pastor has promised to bring about specific solutions, to which he will legalistically hold him, or does he appreciate the pastor's attitude of helpfulness, open-endedly?

It will have dawned on the reader that the variables I am proposing are neither static factors whose presence or absence is to be ascertained, nor measurable factors whose particular loading or intensity is to be found. I see them rather as multidimensional themes which, in the mind of the pastoral interviewer, provide vistas of the person's organization of meanings, at multiple levels and with greater or lesser cohesiveness. They allow both the pastor and his client, in purposeful conversation, to grapple with the psychoanalytic principle of overdetermination. They are meant to give glimpses of how beliefs and over-beliefs are situated in an individual's life, how they affect his thoughts, feelings, and acts, and his perception of his predicaments. They also throw light on the attitudes that prevail in the helping relationship itself.

This is pointedly evident in regard to the third variable I want to present. I can find no better name for it than *faith*, understood subjectively. Its relation to any particular faith, to *the Faith* as an objective and historical pattern of tenets, is to be investigated rather than taken for granted. (A chaplain reported to me that he had heard a psychiatrist describe a patient as having the "fantasy that Christ is his Savior and that he has surrendered his life to Christ." This patient merely described his formal faith content, commensurate with his confession, rather than a personal fantasy.) The diagnostic use of the faith variable lies in guiding the interview and the pastor's observations to the person's affirming or negating stance in life, to his enthusiasm or lukewarmness. Is the person typically a hearty yea-sayer to ideals and the general pattern of reality and life, or does he

tend to be a critical, cautious naysayer, full of ifs, buts, and
howevers? Does he embrace life and experience, or does he
shy away from them?

Even Sartre,[29] a self-designated atheist, speaks of good
faith and bad faith, and makes much of engagement. The
question is not only to what a person commits himself, but
whether he can commit himself at all, whether he is, generally
speaking, *engaged.* Tillich would ask whether he has the
courage to be;[30] James would note whether he has the will to
believe.[31] Jesus would ask about the power of faith. The
particular words used are not so important, but the dispositions of any help-seeking person are of great moment. One is
willing to take risks and may love adventure; another seeks a
safe retreat or maximal disengagement. Some have courage
despite their anxiety; some are just scared to death. To the
pastor's gentle remark "You seem rather timid," one person
may bow his head even farther, while another pricks up his
ears and suddenly mobilizes some dormant energy.

There is an important relation between faith and "the
Faith" which is caught in such expressions as "My faith tells
me . . . ," "I want to hold on to my faith," or "My faith left
me in the lurch." These phrases bespeak a possessive,
anxious, and often defensive use of one's belief system as if it
were an external thing which the person hangs on to, to be
used as a security blanket, lawbook, bulwark, or protector.
One prevailing global symbol for all these features is the
Bible, or, in the client's often repeated phrase, "My
Bible . . . ." Call it bibliolatry if you wish, the diagnostic
value of that symbol of faith lies in what it does to the
person's horizon. Does it open up the world for him, or does
it draw narrow boundaries, making a little niche for an area of
safety? Does it enlarge the person himself, activating all his
talents and stimulating his curiosity, widening the scope of his
engagement, or does it put him into a straitjacket, stifling him

and constricting his abilities? Does he dare venture into learning, science, art, social action, or does he confine himself to *nihil obstat* literature, and the sociability of church basements? He may compartmentalize himself to intercourse with like-minded, like-thinking, like-instructed, and like-molded people in a small, small world, beset by fears of strangers. In other words, this dimension of faith says much about the person's openness or constriction, which are important factors in planning the desirable or workable pastoral interventions. To promote greater openness may itself be the ultimate goal of intervention.

The fourth variable I propose is *grace* or *gratefulness*. As to its best name, almost any cognate or derivative of the Latin *gratia* is worth considering (grace, graciousness, gratitude, gratefulness). They all have something to do with kindness, generousness, gifts, the beauty of giving and receiving, or "getting something for nothing." Whatever his specific theology of grace, the pastor is bound to meet troubled people on precisely that plane of experience where grace is of dynamic importance. In situations beset by guilt feelings, the relevance of forgiveness is obvious. But its specific application is not always so clear, for some people experience considerable tension between their need to be forgiven and their private judgment about their own forgivableness. Some are indeed refractory to grace, no matter how freely offered, and maybe even to the "irresistible grace" of some theologians. In finding themselves unworthy of forgiveness, they may labor under a conviction still greater than their load of guilt feelings: the conviction that they themselves are the final arbiter of their condition and that no higher, wiser, or more ultimate judgment is imaginable. In other words, a large treasure of pride hides behind the wailing wall of their misery, an insistence on the finality of their own self-rejection—in my jargon, a large and potent core of narcissism.

In some cases, excessive narcissism takes the form of not feeling any need for grace or having any gratefulness whatsoever. "Who, me? I don't need anyone's forgiveness." "I have never asked for anything but what people owe me." "Well, yes, I have had much success, but I worked hard for every bit of it." Feelings like these may also come through in the person's opening gambit to his pastor in the interview situation: "I want to see you because that's what I understand you are here for." Everything is a matter of rights or exchanging wares.

Oddities may also appear on the other side—the lady who protests that she is "so thankful . . ." in the midst of excruciating problems, or the man who cannot swear—use theological language from the heart—in his torment. No, they have been taught always to be grateful, to say "thank you" to every neighbor, policeman, or shopkeeper, and even to pray for their enemies. Their gratefulness is an imposed must, an order from their conscience with the knife on their neck. Whatever this forced gratitude is, it has a conspicuous lack of spontaneity and honesty. It shows no trace of the playful friendliness inherent in the word "grace." It is a grim business.

The interviewing pastor is not advised to ask, "Tell me, what are your thoughts about grace?" or, "Where do you stand in relation to question number five of the Catechism?" But he has marvelous opportunities to ask a troubled person, "You just mentioned God—does he ever seem to smile?" Or, if the person's litany of woes appears overdone or prepossessing, he may ask, "Have you thought of how much pain there is everywhere?" Or he may, if he finds it appropriate and feels spontaneous about it, stretch out his hand and give a tender blessing to a person who feels utterly maligned or deprived. In so doing, or in just saying, "Poor man . . . ," he would demonstrate grace right in the helping situation by tapping the source which he and his office symbolize.

I have elsewhere[32] expressed my belief that many troubled people want to be blessed but dare not, or do not know how to, ask for it. I am also sure that some pastors, caught up in their own feelings of anger or frustration, do not want to give a blessing, feeling that their client does not deserve it. That attitude is, in my judgment, quite odd for a pastor. It demonstrates how useless he finds his basic science of theology, which surely defines grace as a free gift. It is not to be dispensed or withheld by considerations or merit. If pastors would feel free and disposed to bless more often, in whatever way, they might discover also its diagnostic value. Who will accept such blessings heartily and gratefully? Who will submit to them with compunctions, who will resist them, who will place himself cockily above them? Who will be moved to tears, who will be gladdened, who will receive, as it were, new energies for tackling his problems? We are now much in the dark about these questions, out of misplaced timidity on both sides.

For the fifth variable the best name is *repentance*, especially the verb *repenting*. It refers to a process of change, most often self-initiated from a condition of felt displeasure or anguish, aimed at a state of greater well-being. Morally, the process can be described as one of correction, from crookedness to rectitude. Soteriologically, it is the process of change from sinfulness to saintliness or from damnation to salvation. It is obviously a very complex variable, but one that lends itself to diagnostic differentiations.

I imagine that one of the first things any pastor would like to know about persons seeking help is their awareness of themselves as agents in the problems they face. The self is an agent in fair and bad times. This is recognized in the old-fashioned phrase "awareness of sin." Highly ritualized in the sacrament of confession, this awareness is to be verbalized and communicated. The next step is a feeling of contrition eventuating in willingness to do penance, which is aided by the anticipated effects of absolution. The whole series of mental activities is an instance of what the psychotherapeutic literature describes as "working through." Whether the pastor is seen as a father confessor or not, he does face analogous processes of problem-solving, crisis resolution, and working through, and gains leverage from the person's inclination toward repentance. Hence his need to be alert to its presence or absence, and its particular forms.

Sorriness for sin presupposes the shouldering of some responsibility for one's problem situation. Does the person assume any responsibility at all? Or does he present himself as a pure victim of circumstances, or fate, not responsible and unaccountable for his misfortune? Or, if he feels that he was a prey to circumstances, does he assume any responsibility for his subsequent internal or external reaction to his plight? Does he feel unduly smitten, playing up the role of passive victim, or does he feel unduly angry, spinning fantasies of revenge? If so, does he feel some sorriness for those patterns of response? Or does he present himself in the most blasé manner, denying any role in his problem, and finding nothing in himself to work on toward betterment? Smugness is not confined to situations of comparative well-being—one can also be smug in his troubles.

In contrast, any experienced pastor knows of persons who seem to assume too much responsibility for their problems, considering themselves the sole agent of their predicament. They are too sorry for debatable sins. Their awareness of sin is pervasive. Since this happens rather often in upstanding citizens and pillars of the church, this hyper-repentance tends to have a phony quality, which bespeaks perhaps a delusional

69129

awareness of sin which does not match with the objective facts. It may stem from a hypertrophy of conscience which sees sin everywhere and is blind to grace. Normal persons are puzzled how such a state can be endured, until it dawns on the observer that behind the woeful facade may lie secret satisfaction at being the "greatest of all sinners." That is a dignified distinction, after all, for some proud souls who find in themselves nothing else to boast of. What I have described here is a dynamic strand in scrupulosity, an old bugaboo of experienced priests.

Remorse, regret, sorrow—these are the feelings one is looking for, particularly in interpersonal conflicts, such as in marriage difficulties and divorce counseling. Does remorse lead to repentance? Does either of the parties feel contrite, i.e., broken in spirit? Does each assume a fair share of responsibility, so that the contrition is joint? Does either have any compunction, any feeling of uneasiness from having heard the voice of conscience? That might be the beginning of repentance, which every pastor is in such exquisite position to aid constructively by the symbols of faith. He does not have to shout, "Repent!" as the prophets of yore. But if he is to guide the process of repentance toward a constructive end he'd better make sure he has some diagnostic estimate of the person's inclination toward repentance, and the idiosyncratic form that process is likely to take for the individual.

We come now to the sixth variable: *communion*. This is a wide-ranging theme, running the gamut from "where two or three are gathered" to having a feeling for patterns of kinship with the whole chain of being, as exemplified in Schweitzer's reverence for life. It has to do with embeddedness, reaching out, caring, and feeling cared for. I do not mean by it a strictly denominational or sectarian belongingness or active membership in a local church. Those are only special forms of communion which may be so encapsulating that they do violence to the idea. I would rather start with that humble, compassionate, and organic sense of communion that allows a person to say, "We are all poor sinners" even when that acknowledgment becomes amplified by aligning oneself with the "company of the faithful."

Perhaps the most basic aspect of the sense of communion is the individual's disposition to see himself either as continuous or discontinuous with the rest of mankind and nature. The first position is analogous to embracing, the second to warding off. I think that this basic choice of emotional response also affects a person's style of thought. Saint Francis felt kinship with nature as a whole, and could sincerely converse with Brother Sun and Sister Moon, whereas most existentialists and men like Eric Hoffer[33] see discontinuity everywhere, proudly arrogating for themselves a distinction from the rest of nature. They refuse to allow any comparison between men and other primates, and often divide mankind itself sharply into authentic and inauthentic creatures.

And so the diagnostic task is to assess whether a person feels fundamentally embedded or estranged, open to the world or encapsulated, in touch or isolated, united or separated. While the alienated may have some company in their isolation or estrangement, which gives them solace, a general attitude of critical cautiousness is likely to prevail, possibly mixed with a good deal of pride. Theirs is not the capacity to say, "There but for the grace of God go I," for such an acknowledgment can stem only from a profound sense of communion.

In the pastoral helping situation one faces the specific embeddedness of a person within his faith group and local church. It is, after all, the latter unit to which a person turns when he seeks a pastor's help. This is also true of those one step removed from this, as in the case of a prison inmate or hospital patient's turning to the institution's chaplain. Yet it is precisely within the faith group or local church that persons may experience a keen sense of alienation, as every pastor knows. Some sense of communion with the wider world may be present, but bitterness prevails toward the small group by which the person feels let down or wounded in some way, leading to an aversive reaction. I think such feelings are rampant today because of the polarizing tendencies that beset the churches, such as liberal versus conservative views, theologies of private salvation versus those of corporate redemption, or the felt distance between national and local church. Alienation from one's own local group tends to be felt more keenly and painfully than estrangement from more distant groups because it involves persons known from face-to-face contacts, thus resembling sibling strife.

Religious beliefs operate simultaneously at two levels in such forms of alienation. A person may break away from the local group, while maintaining a felt sense of communion with the national church if he feels content with its general direction. He may force himself on theological grounds to be ecumenically aligned with untold others elsewhere, who are unfortunately outside his daily orbit. This is one way in which the institutional church sometimes breeds lonely souls, despite its proclamations of brotherhood. I have the vague impression that pastors meet such persons with increasing frequency in their offices and may not know how to respond to them. I also have the impression that certain pastors feel exactly this kind of alienation from their local church themselves, and all the more keenly because they have professionally little freedom to act on those feelings. At any rate, patterns of estrangement within church life require accurate diagnostic assessment, as free as possible from the pastor's own countertransference reactions, for adopting the counseling strategy best suited to promote a felt sense of communion.

Growing feelings of alienation and isolation often become doubly painful because of a sense of guilt of shame. Despite the primacy of the person's experience of estrangement, he may know that having such feelings is somehow wrong, according to his own ethical precepts or his vision of the church. To spot this complex also requires fine pastoral diagnostic acumen. In this condition the pastor will sooner or later have to enter into a thoughtful alliance with the viable aspects of the person's conscience if the problem is to be resolved.

In all these situations I would stress the wisdom of patient and alert listening to the client lest the pastor fall into the trap of defensive arguing. If he knows that the first part of his job is to be diagnostic, the pastor will temper his therapeutic furor sufficiently to forgo serious strategic mistakes. If his counseling is to be successful, he will have to approach some cases with great warmth and compassion, others with strictness, and still others perhaps with sharp confrontation. As Hiltner says of Ichabod Spencer's mishandled case with the distraught woman, "Instead of needing more 'conviction of sin,' she actually needed to have her 'broken heart' bound up." [34] One can only tell one need from the other by making a diagnosis and taking the time to do so, within a consistent conceptual framework.

The seventh theme I propose is *sense of vocation.* By this I do not mean career choice or study goals, but a person's willingness to be a cheerful participant in the scheme of creation and providence, so that a sense of purpose is attached to his doings which validates his existence under his Creator. To some ears, this statement will have the ring of the Puritan ethic as a social model; to others it is a variant of Calvin's image of man in a state of "effectual calling." I am proposing it as a diagnostic variable because of its mid-range position on the ladder of abstraction, which allows it to mediate between high-level theological propositions and the pedestrian details of everyday life. It offers mediation between the various surplus meanings of the word "work," recognizing Luther's differentiation between work in the singular and works in the plural. Add to this Freud's dictum that loving and working are the two most effective ingredients of mental health, and one will find this variable of vocation hardly avoidable as a pastoral diagnostic construct.

The important question is not, "What kind of work do you do, Mr. Jones?" That is only a social inquiry. The pastoral evaluation of vocation starts approximately at the level of Studs Terkel's recent book,[35] composed of interviews with workers of all kinds who are talking about what they do, why they do it, and what satisfactions and frustrations they find in their jobs. In fact, Terkel's book itself can be seen as a casebook for any theology of vocation. It shows most people making an amazing investment in their jobs and approaching their work, however miserable or boring it may be, with a profound sense of vocation. They make their work fit into a set of values and tend to endow it with almost cosmic significance, no matter how lowly the task. If such attitudes prevail in daily labor as much as Terkel's interviews suggest, the pastor should feel emboldened to assess people's posture toward life as a whole, in work and leisure, from the angle of the sense of vocation.

Zest, vigor, liveliness, dedication—these are some direct signs of involvement. But they can all be in the service of destructiveness. Torturers may have all four to a spectacular degree. What sets vocation, theologically understood, apart from just any work or activity? Former ages stressed perfection and obedience to duty; today we may put the emphasis on heartfelt participation in constructive work that is cued to divine benevolence and assiduously shuns alignment with malevolence. A sense of vocation implies alertness to the demonic element in human nature and human affairs, and the desire to control it. Vocation is melioristic—it is putting one's talents to work as a participant in the process that moves the universe toward increasing integrity.

With such a sense of vocation, if only at some crucial moments in life, the life-span of a person attains the quality of a journey and the process of living is endowed with manifold meanings, without which it would be only a dreadful, boring, and fatiguing grind. Life becomes a pilgrimage.

With diagnostic acumen, the pastor will see enormous individual differences in people's sense of vocation from which he will get clues to his interventions. This variable cannot simply be noted as present or absent on a checklist. It evolves into stylistic patterns of experiencing life, of deploying one's energies and coping with its stresses.

Very little observational power is needed to note that styles of experiencing vary between richness and stinginess. In the rich posture, the person stands ready to assimilate much from his world, to say yes to a wide range of experiences and to enjoy much of it heartily. In extreme intensity, this may lead to looseness, insatiable hunger for more or lack of discrimination, and run the risk of odd, syncretistic mixtures of incompatible values and beliefs. In this context, the sense of vocation becomes identified with great expenditure of energy that may be wild and thoughtless. In the stingy posture the emphasis is on caution, purity, and precision, which in effect lead to saying no to many actual or potential experiences. Control is the watchword, and if it is overdone, much of life, experience, and feeling is warded off in one way or another. The risk in that stance is great constriction which channels the sense of vocation into an unproductive perfectionism.

There is another set of stylistic qualifiers to the sense of vocation for which I like to propose the words "humor" and "gravity," both in a broad sense. On the side of humor I would place the willingness to stick out one's neck in curiosity and with imagination, to engage playfully in the diversity of one's vast surroundings, and if gifted, to come with inventive solutions to tasks and problems. Toward the gravity pole of the continuum we find dogmatism in any sense, dedication to the letter rather than the spirit of anything, and a rather grim approach to vocation which makes it a chore or duty that cannot be avoided (for there are textual proofs to show its necessity), but which is fundamentally unpleasant. "Spirit" and "spontaneity" are close to humor, and whimsicality may be their common danger. "Stuffiness" and "heaviness" are close to gravity, with grimness as common danger.

I am sure that more differentiations can be added to capture the individual differences of the sense of vocation. The point of my sketch is that the idea of vocation as I have tentatively circumscribed it sits, as it were, strategically between the various theological doctrines of man and the concrete, messy details of everyday life, and thus provides diagnostic vistas. "What do you really want to do with your life?" the pastor may ask. "What should I do?" the client may respond. One ancient client, known as a rich young man, asked, "Master, what shall I do . . . ?" These are all questions of vocation. They comprise the sixty-four-dollar question about the congruence between life-style and value system.

VI

THE DIAGNOSTIC PARTNERSHIP

I offer these variables as a provisional set of guidelines to steer the pastoral diagnostic interview and help structure the pastor's comprehension of the troubled person before him. A medieval tinkerer with words once turned Pilate's question, *"Quid est veritas?"* into the anagram *"Est vir qui adest"*—"It is the man before you." [36] To grasp that individualized, idiosyncratic truth and to do so compassionately seems to me the substance of diagnosis. But I would like to give it a Whiteheadian dimension. The contact between knower and known, subject and object, is not a unilateral grasp in which an active grasper seizes a passive datum, but a mutual "prehension" arising from and leading to feelings. In prehension, a datum becomes an occasion, a new concrescence within the world's creative advance. Knower and known interpenetrate, they exchange with each other and enrich each other, particularly at organic levels.

This means to me that in those forms of human intercourse where help is pointedly sought and offered, the person seeking help is already on the road toward articulating some understanding of himself. He is already taking stock of himself, he has already begun to diagnose himself by seeking some prospective helper. In selecting one kind of helper rather than another he is already channeling the diagnostic process in a certain direction. He seeks a particular diagnostic perspective, the one that he hopes will benefit him. In offering himself as a "datum" (in Whitehead's sense), he expects to move into an "occasion" where certain feelings germane to himself and the other party will predominate. And so, in coming to a pastor, the client has already made a tentative self-diagnosis which he wishes to explore and articulate further. He expects counsel and advice, to be sure, but he will balk at its coming too early or abruptly, for he first wants to test his self-evaluations with a friend whose perspective he finds congenial or rewarding. He may also balk at its coming in a terminology foreign to the perspective he sought. Disappointed or irritated, he might, if he were blunt, shout at his pastor, "Shoemaker, stick to your last!"

Note that I have offered entrenched religious words having theological coinage without being overly technical. They are not psychological words, although they lend themselves to explorations of experience that can point up marked individual differences. I have not offered a religious typology, or any other classification system. I have not produced a checklist or behavior inventory. Nor have I laid down a pattern for a structured interview.

I have deliberately shied away from these options because I take a dim view of the diagnostic practices that prevail in psychology and psychiatry, and I see no reason for pastors to emulate them. All too often, diagnosing amounts to an act of mere labeling, of sticking a name onto something which makes one feign to know and understand it. Or it means choosing a word or phrase from a list purporting to contain classes of entities, with the implication that each class represents a solid bit of reality with clear boundaries between it and other classes, and that all classes together constitute the universe of entities for a given discipline. I am weary of the professional habit of summing up complex, fluid, and open-ended human conditions in one word, particularly when that word is a noun. Even more so when it is an artificial noun claiming prestige from pseudo-Greek and pseudo-Latin trappings.

Diagnostic word usage in medicine is shaky enough. For instance, the term "appendicitis" has some precision and signal value in that it suggests at least the locus of disorder and something of the process, that it is an inflammation. The cause, however, is not specified in the name. In such a word as "neuralgia," neither locus, nor process, nor cause is fixed—all it suggests is a pain in nerve endings somewhere. In "central nervous system syphilis" a known cause is implied, namely, spirochetes; a process of invasion is postulated, but without known point of entry; the locus is vague—all we know is that the little monsters are hiding somewhere, and the course of illness may be so varied and protracted that it is hard to tell when the patient is phenomenologically ill and when he is not. It is even harder to decide whether the person is to be considered "really ill" when he happens to be symptom-free. These few examples show what tremendous range of known and unknown factors, overt and covert happenings, facts and inferences, data and speculations, certainties and guesses are capsuled in medical designations.

The names for disorders in psychiatry are even shakier. Some, such as "hysteria," are frankly metaphorical or mythical, with a false suggestion of locus. Others, such as "schizophrenia," consist of an allegorical use of common words, "splitting" and "mind" (originally "midriff"), with exquisite looseness or poetic license. Newer words such as "borderline" carry spatial connotations totally out of place in conceptions of mind. Still other words such as "anxiety reaction" are purely descriptive, whereas "depression" and "paranoia" are merely prestige terms for the descriptive words "great sadness" and "unwarranted suspiciousness."

No, naming won't do. Labeling is pernicious, and the vocabularies of medicine and psychiatry are such a problem to these disciplines themselves that they have nothing to recommend themselves to members of other disciplines. A person and his problem cannot and should not be summed up in a word or typological phrase. What we need in the helping professions is a thoughtful formulation of presented problems that combines description with explanation, so worded as to provide clues for feasible intervention. Moreover, that formulation should be arrived at through partnership of the helper and the helped. Ideally it should be so worded that the client or patient can understand it so as to feel free, on the basis of that understanding, to contract for a definable meliorative process. The person is entitled to define for himself, with the help of the expert he seeks out, the nature of his condition, his situation, his self, in the perspective which he finds most relevant.

The variables described in the previous chapter are recognizably based on my own theological intuitions coupled with explicit clinical-psychological knowledge. That combination is vulnerable, not only because it is idiosyncratic but because of the intuitive nature of the implied theology and its selectivity. I am not a systematic theologian, and therefore I have not consciously striven to derive my variables from a particular corpus of dogmatics. I do not pretend that what I have cautiously called "variables" are in any sense systematic categories.

My reluctance to be more definite stems in the first place from being aware of the limitations of the consultant's role. In this case, that role is played by a person at home in psychology, but standing momentarily close enough to psy-

chology's border to take a curious look at theological and
pastoral neighbors, and to strike up a serious conversation
with them. But my reluctance stems from other sources as
well. As Hiltner has been at pains to point out to me,
innovative endeavors can rarely be puristic. Great theologians do not use only theological and, if they are Jewish or
Christian, Biblical truths, but combine these with their
understanding of propositions and trends in other disciplines.
Augustine knew a great deal of ancient psychology, as his
theory of memory shows, and even more about rhetoric.
Thomas Aquinas knew Aristotelian metaphysics in and out,
and used it freely in his theological works. Great psychologists tend to be quite well versed in subject matter of a
different order, including, in the case of William James,
philosophy and theology. Great psychiatrists know far more
than psychiatry alone, as Freud's writings so amply show.
Efforts to guard the uniqueness of a particular perspective
must face the reality principle, which teaches that almost all
perspectives consist of subtle interdisciplinary combinations
which yield various figure-and-ground patterns.

Therefore, my calling attention to professional specificity
should not be taken to mean that pastors should use nothing
but theology in their work, that physicians should never
deviate from medicine, and that psychiatrists should unwaver-
ingly confine themselves to the hard-won facts of their
discipline and use nothing else. This whole treatise is, after
all, addressed to *professional* people who, unlike their coun-
terparts in the purely academic and basic research domains,
are acutely aware of the tremendous influence that practice
and skill have on basic theory. For professional people,
"doing" constantly informs and transforms "knowing." In
actual professional operations, the perspectives are always
somewhat mixed—they always have some interdisciplinary
tinges. But it is incumbent upon any professional person to

know what his particular mix of perspectives is, and how he ranks their importance in his work, so as not to confuse the origins and anchorage points of his thoughts and actions.

The diagnostic partnership between pastor and parishioner, then, evolves from two parties, each with a set of expectations and habitual outlooks, coming together to engage in a process of problem-solving. The pastor is a professional person, trained to look at things in a theological and ethical perspective and to assume certain attitudes emphasized by his tradition. By social fiat he has been given the right of access and initiative, which he can exercise in various ways. But that right is coupled with a duty. He must be, among other professionals, a highly accessible resource to whom people can turn without much formality. He has a great many pastoral "tools" which he can selectively apply to suitable situations. He may, in addition, have appropriated varying degrees of knowledge and skills originally developed in other professions, now more or less assimilated into his pastoral framework of thought and operations. The other party, the help-seeking parishioner, brings to the occasion his problem-laden self, his troubles, his panic, his despair, his failing sense of direction, or what not—plus one or more of the attitudes and expectations described in Chapter IV. Among these is the expectation that the pastor will bring the resources of his office to bear upon the personal troubles that are now to be shared. There is also the spoken or unspoken hope that the perspective of faith will at least bring out some special dimensions of the person's predicament that are not so readily grasped in other perspectives.

The parishioner is likely to bring to the encounter with the pastor many other attitudes and feelings. He may expect magic from "the man of God." If the parishioner is a woman, she may have a crush on the pastor, childishly hoping that some of her erotic wishes will be fulfilled. He or she may

relate to pastors in general with great ambivalence, extolling
and needling them in surprising and intricate combinations.
The person's relation to his faith, tradition, or local church
may be tenuous in some way, giving the plea for help an
argumentative, feisty, or condescending tone. The person's
attitude may be overly dependent, competitive, exploitative,
overly pious, even unctuous. All these are what psychothera-
pists call transference patterns, consisting, broadly speaking,
of transferring old relationship patterns with parents, ac-
quired in childhood, onto the new relation to the pastor, who
is now seen, falsely, as a parentlike figure. Transference
besets the relation to the pastor with inappropriate or false
expectations, no matter whether these are pleasantly or
unpleasantly toned. These expectations are likely to become
traps in the helping process if they are not recognized for
what they are and what their origin is.

On the other hand, the whole combination of conscious
and unconscious anticipations of the help-seeking person
provides the ideal setting for pastoral assessment of the
troubled person and for cementing the two parties into a
diagnostic partnership. In that partnership the parishioner is
to be addressed with the kind of respect that grants the need
for stocktaking, for deciphering the presented problem within
the framework of expectations, whether tenable or untenable,
that brought this person to his or her pastor. The partnership
is responsible for placing the problem in the special perspective (modulated by ancillary perspectives) in which pastors,
representing the church, have expertise.

Pastors do a great variety of things and function ordinarily
with great diversity of roles. Although their office is represen-
tational in many different ways and at diverse levels, including a level of cosmic significance, they are not jacks-of-all-
trades. Nor are they seen in this way, other than jocosely, by
the parishioners who turn to them for help. They are, if

anything, a little awesome, lifted somewhat above the ordinary. Though it may be difficult to define exhaustively in what way they are unique, pastors have for ages rightly been regarded as experts in a special way of looking at man, his place in nature and society, and his role as creature. Keenly or dimly, parishioners know this and therefore endow their help-seeking visits to pastors with a special tone to which they fully expect a harmonious response. Undoubtedly, my own intuitive theology will come through in offering the thought that the deepest, ultimate motive driving persons to pastors rather than other helpers and caretakers is a realization of their own creatureliness, and a desire to be regarded in that special dimension of their humanity. In my opinion the unique integrity of pastoral diagnostic work rests upon recognizing this, and acting on it.

VII

LANGUAGE IN
THE PASTORAL RELATIONSHIP

In comparison with other disciplines, especially the helping professions, theology is in a unique position in regard to its use of language. Its crucial words have for years been shared with the public through sermons, books, lessons, hymns, and rituals. Its primary source of vocabulary, the Holy Scriptures, has been the property of the masses since the Reformation. Moreover, that primary source is not a textbook propounding a conceptual system, as the source books of other disciplines are and do, but a collection of literary pieces as diverse as poetry and genealogical tables, myth and historical narrative, letters and visionary prophecies.

Some rarefied technical expressions such as "eschatology" and "soteriology" are the privilege of learned specialists. Theology's borrowings from philosophy, such words as "ontological," "*summum bonum,*" or "categorical imperative," are not well known to laymen. However, the basic words of theology and its pastoral applications have common coinage and find many illustrative reference points in Scripture—indeed, in much of Western literature and the arts. This common coinage does not bar misunderstanding, to be sure, but most of the words are part of the public vocabulary. They do not sound strange or forbidding. They are found in

Webster's Dictionary, on tombstones, in songs, in marriage vows, on mothers' lips, and with great profusion in Texas radio broadcasts. They are peddled in a million pamphlets and fund-raising schemes. Their familiarity is almost embarrassing, and this may be one reason why some self-conscious pastors shy away from their use. But in so doing, they also shy away from some of their parishioners.

Not so in the other disciplines. Their textbooks are by and large for the learned and the initiated, the researchers and practitioners. From the start their key words are technical, conceptual, and sometimes arcane—they can be grasped only after considerable exposure or technical involvement. While certain elites may wrest these words from their proper moorings for use at cocktail parties or in "hip" forms of journalism, such a term as "penis envy" has little to do with inebriation, and "schizophrenia" is not an appropriate description of politics in Southeast Asia. Nor is "Puritan ethic" the right term for just any concept of hard work. "Symbiotic" is grossly out of place as a mere allusion to a mother and her child, and the family therapist's "triadic" is not just another word for a family of three. The great false prestige of all these technical terms seems to endear them, as long as fads last, to various upstarts.

Moreover, theologians are trained to be exegetes. Whatever their hermeneutic principles, they are seen as able translators and interpreters who can clarify complex passages for the common man and woman, who are themselves in most essential respects much like the people that populate the pages of the basic literary resource, the Scripture. Among theologians, the practicing pastors are also trained in homiletics, the art of purposeful speaking in which ordinary words are repolished to attain brilliance of meaning. Difficult propositions come through as an understandable, personal message. Of all people in the helping professions, the pastors should be the best raconteurs, the clearest interpreters, and the least prone to the use of technical jargon. Granted that all this training in right talking may make them poor listeners, any good course in counseling can disabuse a pastor of excessive verbal narcissism while preserving for his use a marvelous common language bond with his clients.

I am dwelling on these features of pastoral and religious language for a reason. Our generation of scholars has been told by learned men that theological language is particularly nonsensical, spurious, fatuous, deceptive, nonempirical, unfalsifiable, mythical—and a host of other denigrating epithets current in the ambiance of Oxford and Cambridge.[37] I do not deny the validity of such critical arguments, but I question their potency. I do not think they make a scratch or a dent in the word usage of any ordinary believer. They do not affect people's love for hymns, not even their irrational preference for bad hymns, such as William Cowper's:

> There is a fountain filled with blood
>   Drawn from Emmanuel's veins;
> And sinners, plunged beneath that flood,
>   Lose all their guilty stains.

Yes, in religious and pastoral language we have to do with symbol words, and while we may like to be cautious with these, we should not put a ban on their use in any pastoral setting. If the pastor throws his symbol words overboard, he has no cargo left, and his ship will yaw. One hard blow of the wind and it will sink. Whatever refinements theological language may have to undergo, it does not have to dispense with its uniqueness by sacrificing its symbols. The full life requires many languages and the skill to move from one to the other; it does not benefit from an Esperanto-style leveling process.

Here is an example of a pastoral diagnostic sentence about a nun, hospitalized for mental illness:

"She is in the very painful position of having invested over twenty years in a religious vocation and in commitment to a God who has abandoned her at her time of greatest need."

Compare it with a psychiatric sentence about the same patient:

"Having been forced over the years to cathect only one object, she now feels keenly ambivalent toward it, i.e., 'God,' because her magical hope for betterment is not fulfilled."

Is it fair to ask which of these you prefer? The answer depends initially on one's frame of reference. The first statement is pastoral, the second psychiatric; neither is particularly stunning. We will feel at home with one or the other according to our profession. I must add, however, that the pastoral phrase with its unabashed use of God as Person, without quotation marks, adds liveliness and depth of experience to the problem formulation. And the patient would immediately recognize it as pertaining to herself—she may remember exactly what she said in that interview with the chaplain. I doubt that she would recognize herself promptly in the psychiatric statement.

As I remarked before, pastors are sometimes wary about the God-talk of their clients, going out of their way to avoid it themselves. This can give rise to odd exchanges and interactions. I remember a young Roman Catholic priest, then being trained in pastoral counseling in a parish setting. In his zeal for social ethics, he had grown suspicious of the common believer's symbol language, shrugging it off as piosity. He met his nemesis in a middle-aged married woman who told him in the first interview that she wanted to know the will of God for herself in a difficult situation. A late convert to Roman Catholicism, she went regularly to confession, but always found that she was not given enough time, which estranged her somewhat from the church. It took a session with a

visiting priest to straighten out that chronic disappointment.
Now she was in a special fix: Her alcoholic husband had taken
to Alcoholics Anonymous, and she, as his wife, had begun to
attend sessions also. In these she had felt a sense of
communion more profound than she had ever felt in her
church. Who of the two was right—the church or AA? And
were not the principles of AA grounded in the Bible also?
She felt desperate. What did God want her to do? Indeed, it
was God who had told her to go see her priest. Somewhere in
the first interview the following interchange occurred, which
is more like a parry than an encounter:

Woman: I thought by talking with you, you could give me the
         answer.
Priest: And now you are not quite sure I can do that?
Woman: What?
Priest: You're not sure I have the answer?
Woman: I can find the answer—God has all the answers.

The woman insists on using her religious symbols and expects
that the priest will fall in with this usage. He does not. He
ducks it, and gets testy about the role of authority in which
he is being placed. The woman goes on hoping that he will
prove to be a man of God. In subsequent interviews she
keeps at it with increasing vigor. The more he ducks the
issues, the bigger her volleys. No meek character, she finally
tests his priestly sincerity by blatantly falling in love with him
and telling him so, which is quite embarrassing to him. This
leads to a rather abrupt separation as she turns, seemingly
without compunction, to the arms of AA. The young man, in
wanting to be a counselor, refused to be a priest. He also
became unable to act as a priest because he himself was
infected, as it were, by the woman's intense anxiety. He
never understood what she sought from him.

Such a case is an occasion for some sober questions. Is the client's use of symbol language a bit of superficial role behavior? Sometimes it is. You talk to your pastor about faith and God and rules for living as you talk to your psychiatrist about rage and sex and potent feelings that linger on from childhood. In this particular case, could it be a sample demonstration of AA jargon? It might, but this is what the woman seemed to question herself. Could the use of symbol language be a way of hinting at a desire for replies in the same vein? Possibly, but what's wrong with that, especially if you find some depth or relevance in such language—which, moreover, the saints are reported to have also spoken? And could it not be an entirely spontaneous act, without tactical or strategic considerations, as a straightforward affirmation of one's creatureliness, faith, upbringing, or deepest feelings? Of course it can. But we do not know how often such religious spontaneity occurs unless we give its language use a fair chance. Surely the pastoral counselor has to be wise as a serpent and innocent as a dove—both attitudes are needed in his diagnostic work, as they are in all helping professions.

The case elicits further questions. I have not yet mentioned that the young priest sought a psychiatric consultation for himself after the woman had attested to her love for him. In this consultation the man's resistance to acting as a priest was discussed, and in that context he also felt that the case should now be referred to a psychiatrist. When asked why, he emphasized the difficulty of the case, the seriousness of the woman's disorder, his own disabling anxiety, and the high skill needed in helping her. Bracketing what needed to be done for the priest himself, the consultant found referral of the client not only unnecessary, but thought it would be an act of deceptive packaging. The woman had sought pastoral guidance—who were we, priest and consultant, to try talking her into something else? Even the Better Business Bureau would have objected.

Now I must also sound a warning against possible abuses of the language I myself have struck in Chapter V, when I proposed several named diagnostic variables. I introduced words, key words such as *communion, faith, grace.* These words are old and have become rich in meanings by centuries of use. They are, to say the least, rather religious words. Most of them are quite theological in the sense that they occur as chapter headings in books on dogmatics and have prompted questions and answers in catechisms. Therein lies their danger.

Some pastors may have such fondness for these words that they will seek to lard their diagnostic conversations with them. These are precisely the terms that belong in a church office, they will say. They may even feel thankful for the happy circumstance that in this case a psychological consultant advocated their use by pastors. My answer to such declarations of fondness is that I do not advocate the use of these words in diagnostic conversations at all! A social worker does not use the phrase "sibling rivalry" with his client, but simply asks about feelings toward brothers and sisters. A psychoanalyst does not mention "Oedipus complex," but elicits from his patient some awareness of erotic feelings toward parents. And so, by good listening, the pastor may register tones of gratefulness in his parishioner's outpourings, or, by artful conversation, ask whether the person can forgive himself for some failure, without having to enunciate the word "grace." Literalism and fundamentalism in the use of these words are to be avoided.

Other pastors may find the key words that I used handy markers for apportioning specific phases of the pastoral diagnostic process. Trying to be orderly, they may set the first ten minutes of the second interview aside for a discussion of grace, to be followed by fifteen minutes on repentance. Such a literal-methodical approach, which amounts to turning my hints into an organized procedure, would be a gross distortion of my intention. It is true that in medicine, physicians do their physical examinations in an orderly fashion, reviewing step by step the respiratory system, the digestive system, the endocrine system, etc., concretely checking off each observation on a printed examination form. Nothing of this kind fits the pastoral diagnostic process. The key words I proposed are not to be taken as numbered entries on an imaginary questionnaire that one feels under compulsion to fill out.

In what sense then are the words I proposed key words? Are not keys used to open up something? Yes and no. Keys are used to close as well as open. When a pastoral diagnostic conversation gets riddled with theological jargon it is time to close the door on that abuse and settle for a down-to-earth focus on what the parishioner concretely does or feels or wants in the sphere of his day-by-day relations at home or at work. If, on the other hand, a diagnostic conversation is conspicuous by the persistent absence of any allusions, no matter how covert, to the hallowed auspices under which the pastor works (and under which the parishioner feels free to seek him out), it is time to open the door for some encounter with the transcendent. But even this does not require that the pastor actually introduce such words as *vocation, communion,* or *Providence* in his speech.

If the parishioner spontaneously uses one or more of the key words in his conversation, the pastor can tacitly note that fact and, also tacitly, seek to interpret it. He may momentarily tune in to the parishioner's word usage and use the occasion for some exploration of the associations and meanings that these words have to the user.

The words I proposed should *linger in the pastor's mind,*

functioning as guideposts to his diagnostic thinking and as ordering principles for the observations he makes. To a lesser degree, they may alert him to dimensions of experience that thus far have not come to the fore, and which may have to be singled out for discussion. In every diagnostic process there is selective attention as well as selective inattention. Key words and the loose schema they form in the diagnostician's head alert him to the overlooked, forgotten, or inconspicuous dimensions of experience and help him to attain a certain coverage.

I offer these warnings about the use and abuse of my own words with some vigor, because the sense for order and a dedication to "tools" often prematurely give telling words the status of all-sufficient categories. Or they push the user toward taking them as concrete, actual entities that form the real "substance" of one's sphere of interest. Something of this sort has happened to Erikson's[38] *identity, doubt, trust, shame,* etc. Their listing in charts and diagrams of developmental progression superficially suggests that they are as specific to certain age levels as, say, the acquisition of secondary sexual characteristics in puberty. Nothing is farther from the truth. These words stand for perennial themes that are relevant from the cradle to the grave, but their meanings and prominence and combinations vary in highly individual ways. Their longitudinal dimension, it must be noted, gives only one "handle" on their complexity.

Precisely because pastoral work has a holistic tenor, commensurate with the vast sweep of the theological viewpoint, pastors should take caution not to exhaust themselves in methodical minutiae. They must not be slaves to words, not succumb to completeness-compulsion by going over checklists. What counts diagnostically is to size up an image, to get an overall picture which, if it must be a verbal one, is succinct and telling rather than laborious and crammed.

VIII

REASONS FOR REFERRAL

From here on, we can let our fantasy take free rein. Suppose that at this point the woman described in the previous chapter had gone to a psychiatrist. She would probably have said something about having sought priestly counsel, only to be thwarted in that search and learn instead that there must be something unnameably wrong with her. The psychiatrist, tactfully falling in with her language for a moment, might have asked about that "will of God for her," hoping to find something essential about her through that metaphor. Since the case was referred to him by a priest, he would very likely assume that if the priest found her God-talk suspect, it must indeed be very metaphorical, probably a defense against some deep, intolerable fantasies which she finally acted out by falling in love with the counselor during that unhappy series of interviews. How inappropriate! How symptomatic! This shrewd young priest is to be commended for his perspicacity in making a psychiatric referral at the right time!

This is no wild fantasy. It is only a sample of the kind of thing that occurs with some regularity between two groups of helpers, pastors and psychiatrists. I offer it not for a giggle, but to point out the tragic impact it has on the interaction between these two professions, and sometimes on their clientele. Occurrences like this build up the myth that the essential difference between pastoral and psychiatric help is in the degree of skill these professions offer and in the degree of disturbance the help-seeking persons present. Professional specificity is thereby reduced to a quantitative variable, to which other quantitative differences are tacitly added—duration of treatment, fees, the alleged degree of the person's involvement, and the reputed intensity of change to be produced. I find all these differences fictitious. Wherever they come from, they do not follow from the unique knowledge base, skill, or perspective of either profession. Neither do they come from the personal qualities of either kind of practitioner, nor from the prospective clients or patients. Unless, as in the case described, these persons become the pawns in an interprofessional game already loaded with false assumptions.

Now let us fantasize another turn of events which is far less frequent but does occur. The psychiatrist and the woman actually engaged in a therapeutic process from which the patient gained some benefit. Maybe she developed insight into the role she had played in her husband's alcoholism; maybe she learned to cope better with an inherently difficult and unchangeable reality problem. Perhaps she learned to seek some much needed satisfactions of her own, not hinging on her husband. Feeling stronger and more competent, she might have dropped her earlier concern over the will of God. She sought no further pastoral advice. The metaphor "will of God" disappeared from her conversation with the psychiatrist. One may infer from such an outcome that the use of religious symbols by people seeking help demonstrates that theological language is apt for people *in extremis* and serves an ad hoc function. Swearing is another instance of the same order. With increasing sanity and rationality, theological language gives way to other kinds of language, presumably better or clearer or more precise.

We can spin another fantasy. Our woman achieved with the psychiatrist the same general improvement we described before, except that she kept wondering audibly from time to time about the will of God. The psychiatrist, noting her improvement, referred her back for counseling with a priest. Having done for her what he could, yet recognizing that she still sought help, he in turn referred her to a specialist in matters of God's will. Such a referral could have been based on diverse reasons. Pleased with her improvement, the psychiatrist may have felt that she was now much more ready than before to pursue her theological quest and profit from the advice of appropriate specialists. This manner of reasoning makes theological queries and language rather special, for which one needs to meet criteria of readiness, ripeness, health, or openness because of their presumed elevation or difficulty. God-talk is now like high-octane gasoline—it is at a premium.

Another reason for referral to a pastor might be the psychiatrist's conviction that this woman needed some ongoing sustenance, just the kind that in his fantasy churches and their pastors typically offer in readily accessible, friendly, simple, and inexpensive ways. He may have felt she needed shelter, along with a chance to sound out others about the will of God. So he referred her basically for a special ambiance, a comforting place, a safe harbor that could have a lot of fringe benefits for her. Referrals like this from psychiatrists to pastors or churches do occur rather regularly. This reasoning implies that God-talk and theological explorations are all right in their place, in the proper milieu, and in certain cliques. If some of our patients insist on this kind of thing, why withhold it from them? Let them indulge their innocuous fancy. In fact, it may be positively good for them—for their mental health, that is. And so we will at times refer some cases to the church, convinced that it will do some good. Obviously, for such referrals the psychiatrist need not be knowledgeable at all about the specifics of the pastoral perspective. He can go by vague impressions, feeling glad that society has some niches for people who need shelter. In this train of thought, which I find rather patronizing, the theological perspective is neither praised nor blamed, but some of its trappings are opportunistically used. It is spatialized into a sphere or a little country whose borders we ourselves never need to cross. The pastor who receives such referrals is almost put in the role of a travel agent who is asked to make a booking for a nice old lady to the Emerald Isle, with its quaint and enchanting customs.

I can think of still another reason for such a referral. Our patient is grateful to her psychiatrist for the help she has received. She does not feel that her life has eased or that she can cope better with her problems, but she has gained some awareness of her own complexity. What seemed at first a fairly simple problem has now become in her mind a multifaceted and greatly ramified one which cries out for different vantage points. Her curiosity about herself and her life has not been quieted, but greatly stimulated. Pertly, she tells the psychiatrist that she is now more than ever interested in the will of God for her. In fact, she now has some pointed questions about it which she wants to discuss with an expert. Obligingly, the psychiatrist helps her get in touch with her pastor. Or with a lively sense of helpfulness and conviction, he may ask: "Do you know Father So-and-So who is in the Holy Something Church? I've heard very good things about him. He has been helpful to some of my patients." In other words, he is making a positive recommendation for a pointed purpose—he helps the woman find the best possible local expert because he esteems or respects her theological concerns. In fact, he asks the woman whether he may have her permission to call this priest so as to smooth her path toward him and share with him some of the things they have talked about together.

What I am trying to describe here is a pointed, respectful, and skillful referral from one expert to another, unblemished by one-upmanship, by patronizing attitudes, or by denigration of the patient. This psychiatrist knows his business—he has a complex view of personality, he respects the rights of his patients, he esteems his colleagues in the other helping professions, and he wants his patients to grow beyond the level that he himself has helped them achieve. He is capable of multidimensional thinking, and he assumes that other professionals can do the same. Proud of the skill he has within his own perspective and secure in his discipline, he gracefully enlists the potentialities of other perspectives when his patients need these or when they ask for them.

After all these fantasies, one may ask a down-to-earth question: Is it not really up to the client or patient to seek his own resources in the community? Why these referrals? Is not the client or patient his own agent, free to seek what he wants, wherever it may be? On the face of it, I would say yes to these questions, but immediately add a weighty caveat.

Problem-laden people are often bewildered and may at first not know what they want. They may repeatedly change their mind on what they want. And apart from knowing what one wants, help-seeking itself is difficult and requires courage. It involves a testimony of personal defeat, an admission of troubles and perhaps a painful exposure of things one would rather keep secret. Help-seeking is made all the more difficult by the Kafkaesque apparatus of helping professions and agencies in many communities, which makes the question of where to go for help so hard to answer that the first weak impulse at seeking it often becomes stymied. The fragile tendril dies on the vine.

Even worse, among the various helpers themselves can be found considerable provincialism, authoritarianism, or reductionism. Any of these may force even the wide-awake client who knows that his problem is multifaceted into one simplistic groove, where he may remain stuck. The opposite, stemming from the same causes, also occurs. The client finds himself endlessly referred, being passed on from one helper to another like the proverbial buck, without resolving his problem. A telling term in social welfare circles, "multiple problem families," raises an intriguing question. The question is, Where does multiplicity reside? In the client or in the prospective helpers? The term bluntly pluralizes the problem of a family, putting that family in a special category of near-unresolvable predicament. Yet that family's problem may be only one—say, excruciating poverty—to which many different perspectives are relevant. Thus, the bewildering multiplicity of the helping agencies themselves and their typical incoordination become projected on the family, with more or less accusatory overtones. In effect, the helping agencies impose their own fragmentation upon the client.

Small wonder, then, that clients do not always know where to go for the help they seek, and that referrals are a substantial part of many a helper's business. But referring should not be regarded as passing the client on from one's own office to another. If disciplines and professions are perspectives, as I have proposed, certain problems need highlighting in several perspectives at once. A datum can lead to several simultaneous prehensions and become a pattern of several occasions, in Whitehead's sense.

My main reason for emphasizing this multiperspectival approach is that pastors hold a unique position in the referral process. Their perspective has an exceptionally high degree of viability. Some would go so far as to say that their perspective is omniviable, deriving this quality from the omniscience, omnipotence, and omnipresence of the divine constituent with which this perspective is concerned. I would rather point to the less than omnipresent, but quite substantial religious needs of many problem-laden individuals which drive them to the offices of their pastors. Seemingly they hope to have their problems faced and met in pastoral-theological perspective, whatever else may be recommended besides.

And so we have to add one more possibility to our fantasies about the woman who wanted to know the will of God for herself. This woman might have needed both pastoral and psychiatric help at once. The priest may have referred her to a psychiatrist while continuing to see her himself. Why? In the first place, because the woman asked for his advice and help. Whatever else she sought or needed, she was persistently interested in questioning herself theologically. She was entitled to that opportunity, in dignity. In the second place, because the priest learned from the consultant that he had for reasons of his own dodged the woman's desire for priestly advice. He, therefore, had to do a job on himself, trying to come to terms with all the implications of his office. In the third place, I hope, because he himself knew that theology does not deal with a slice of reality but with all of it, always. He had learned belatedly, and through much agony to be sure, what Sartre's Self-Taught Man never learned: that knowledge is not additive, but pluralistic and perspectival.

The conclusion, then, is that there are good and poor grounds for referrals between clergy and psychiatrists, either way. There are helpful books about referral, particularly for pastors deliberating whether or not they should refer a parishioner to a psychiatrist or psychiatric agency. But they are, by and large, imbued with apprehension that the pastor may find himself "over his head" in difficult cases. Or else, they strive to simplify the busy pastor's life by warning him that he cannot bring to a good conclusion every plea for help that comes his way. Both points are sound, and the advice should be heeded. But I have seldom seen the referral process discussed on the basis of principle, professional integrity, and the client's expectations, as I have tried to do through the preceding vignettes.

If knowledge and professions are perspectival, as I hold, and if human problems tend to be as multifaceted, as I think they are, referral of troubled persons from one helping profession to another is to be guided by these considerations. Expediency, deference to someone else's specialized knowledge and skill, awareness of one's own professional or personal limitations, and recognition of the client's most conspicuous needs at the moment are not enough, though they are all very important. By the time help is sought, most people's needs are no longer simple but multidimensional, and that feature has to be fully taken into account.

IX

THE AGAPIC COMMUNITY

There is need now to return to the idea of communion, which I treated earlier as a diagnostic variable. I still stand by my proposal that pastors would do well to explore their parishioners' or clients' sense of, and feelings about, communion for the light these may shed on their problems. But in theological perspective, communion also defines the helping process itself, and gives the pastoral office at large a special value charge. A strong and numinous sense of communion may be one of the key motives for men and women to seek the ministry as vocation in the first place. Once they are launched upon their careers this sacred value will irradiate all their thoughts and doings. It takes only a small verbal step to bundle up these motives, feelings, and values into one word—a word that is not so much a concept as, all at once, a command, an attitude, a proclamation, a state of being, and an ontic affirmation. That word is *agape*.

Communion is not only descriptive, but prescriptive. From this point of view, pastoral work is a labor of love that must be done with competence. But pastoral work is in this special perspective also, as it were, a cornucopia of zestful acts of loving, poured out with spontaneity. And the pastoral setting—the church—is then the concrete reality of men and women on whom this cornucopia is lavished and from whom it constantly replenishes itself. The gathered are gathered to love; the called are called to love; the elect are elected to love. Everybody is to be embedded in communion, for "God is love."

In this atmosphere of thought and feeling, any act of caring or counseling may assume features which my presentation, up to this point, had to "bracket." For much as I personally believe that, in a sense, all pastoral care is providential care mediated, I also know on more evidential grounds that many pastors see their vocation singularly as response to a divine call to a hallowed office. As a consequence they cannot allow themselves to see ministry as a profession. Exclusive concentration on ministry as divine calling has often led to militant opposition to any trace of professionalism, to the "learned" ministry, and to the very idea of a reasoned and reasonable faith. My presentation, such as it is, simply does not and cannot speak to pastors of this extreme persuasion.

Barring this radical position, however, it is also known that many more pastors seek to hold both views of the office in some kind of apposition—they avow that their ministry is both a response to a divine call and a self-chosen profession. To hold this double conviction entails some personal tension and demands tolerance for ambiguity, for in the past these two views have often been seen as antagonistic. Certain current issues in the ministry, such as the willingness to put up with low salaries not commensurate with the duration of academic education, prove that this ambiguity persists. There is also an excessive tolerance by some seminaries for eccentricities and mental illness in theological students, which places a burden on the churches that eventually employ such graduates. It is not easy to hold both a mystical or inspired, and a workmanlike view of the pastoral office in which goodwill and competence are properly blended. But this difficulty also entails a blessing—if that is the right word for it. In moments of tension a pastor can rationalize his lack of professional skill by hiding in the safety zone of the divine call. I do not know how to solve this historical problem, but I do know that because of its lack of resolution the pastor shoulders a unique ambiguity that does not exist in other professions.

At any rate, if this built-in ambiguity of the pastoral office does not feed unduly the pastor's personal ambivalence (from whatever source the latter may stem), the pastor's sense of calling and his cherished value of communion may well give him a special perspective *on* the general perspective of pastoral work with which I have dealt. Subscribing to an inspired view of the call and a theology of communion, he may subordinate the basic technology of his discipline to the Biblical command to love. His personal faith and its agapic charge allow him in reflective moments some distance from his systematic and historic discipline, i.e., from the perspective unique to his vocation.

Some pastors and parishioners alike will say that this special perspective of faith makes heavy demands for the implementation of its prescription. The pastorate requires the best possible training, the most deliberate acquisition of skills, the selection and nurturing of the most competent persons, the most assiduous continuing education of graduate ministers, the freest interaction with other disciplines, the most stringent peer review, and the most ambitious goals for theological education. I align myself with these views without hesitation. But I do not assume that achievement of these goals will set the matter straight, once for all. The perspective of faith which prescribes the nurture of communion highlights an unanalyzable datum which I can only describe as *spontaneity*. I think that spontaneity is divine.

Without it we cannot have a process conception of the universe. To me, whatever God may be, spontaneity defines his essence. But at the human level, spontaneity is a paradoxical thing. You can experience it, but you cannot promote it. If you extol it, you only testify to having lost it. You can go miserably awry in wanting to be spontaneous. If you celebrate spontaneity, you are likely to be prey to a compulsion. "Feast of fools" [39] indeed!

And so the balance between ministry as calling and ministry as profession may hinge upon another balance: the fleeting equilibrations between spontaneity and competence. I cannot and will not systematize my thoughts on this. But I can toy with a picture, a picture of a pastor who goes out and loves.

He will visit in people's homes to demonstrate and nurture communion. He will seek communion in his counseling, he will try to embed in communion the sick, bereft, poor, imprisoned, and oppressed. And he will assume that the people he meets, the people who seek him out, the people who knock at his office door, or who call him at home late at night, are essentially seeking acceptance in a community of love. He will admit that people do not always come to him for help and advice, they do not always seek his expertise in problem-solving, they do not only come to let their hair down, and they do not merely want to engage him as a master of ceremonies in their celebrations. Ask such a pastor what people want, and he will say that above all else they want communion. They want to love and be loved, and they want to know what love is, by engagements with their pastors in the fellowship of their church.

I have nothing to say about this high and noble view, except that it too needs to be tested in the crucible of diagnostic thought. According to the apostle John, even the spirits must be tested.

X

SOME PASTORAL APPLICATIONS

It should be clear from the whole foregoing discourse that I am not a pastor and do not work under the auspices of any church. Hence I can in no way apply my own proposals to the work I do, nor can I test their viability in my diagnostic contacts with patients. I am a psychologist working in a secular psychiatric institution, not beholden to any faith group, nor bound to any theological image of man. In a broad way my concern is with interdisciplinary functioning in the helping professions, in only one of which I hold membership. The latter condition sets strict limits to my own enterprises if I am to be true to the perspectival schema which I have set forth.

More specifically, I have raised the question of how to achieve adequate richness in interdisciplinary helping efforts. As an answer I am holding out for optimal integrity and authenticity of each profession. This answer consists of a double thesis: (1) that each profession must be highly aware of its own knowledge base and applied-science features, and use its skills with utmost competence; 2 that interdisciplinary work is superior to single-discipline approaches only when the specificity of each participating discipline is vouchsafed in a process of pooling or sharing. This leads to cumulative knowledge conducive to the grasping of a larger and more intricate whole than each separate discipline is capable of. This interdisciplinary approach requires, as I have argued, a determination to sharpen rather than level the differences in each discipline. Only thus can richness of understanding be gained. Only thus can the ultimate, multiple needs of the clients or patients be honored. only thus is interdisciplinary practice exciting and stimulating. Only thus can we prevail against identity confusion and diffusion. Only thus can we make sense of the truism that "two minds are better than one."

So I must leave it to pastors—and pastors only—to tinker with my suggestions and try them out in their varied practices. Of what value they are I cannot yet judge—at least not on empirical grounds. Only pastoral practitioners can put their value to the test, by trying to apply these ideas to their diverse work situations and finding out whether they are congenial to their orientation, "feel right," and are pragmatically useful.

Ideally, then, new books and articles should be written *by pastors* on "The Minister as Diagnostician," to verify or contradict, accept or reject, modify or leave intact my proposals. But that is an involved process requiring much time. To ask the reader of this book to wait for its completion, or even its first outcomes, would be unfair.

I have found several friends, all pastors, willing to start the verification process that is needed. With their permission I will now share with the reader their first attempts to put into practice a way of interviewing and reporting that evolves from the pastoral diagnostic guidelines described in Chapter V. The case fragments and vignettes that follow are playful, almost furtive endeavors to "look and see" where diagnostic pastoral interviews would lead if conceptually guided in the interviewer's mind by the proposed variables. How could the results be formulated, and how might they be conveyed to members of other disciplines?

The first three cases to be reported are from a pastor, approaching middle age, who leads a relatively small but vital congregation in a moderate-size city. His church is in close proximity to a college campus. On this account it has quite a few young members and perhaps an unusual proportion of students attending worship only occasionally. The pastor is the sole minister of this church. Because of his amiability, trustworthiness, and dedication he is visited by people seeking help with a great variety of personal problems. He is not specialized as a counselor; his vision and skills as a helper have evolved from his personal bent and standard seminary training, plus years of practical learning in a wide-ranging, diversified ministry.

CASE 1: LAMBERT, A GUILTY COLLEGE STUDENT

While visiting a church school class one morning, I received a note saying that a young man urgently needed to see me. When I stepped out into the hall, the man explained that he had a pressing personal problem about which he needed to talk with me as soon as possible. He is a flashy-appearing, 20-year-old junior at the local university. We arranged to meet in my study late that evening. In our visit that night, he stated that he was deeply upset and unable to concentrate on his studies because his girl friend had terminated their relationship.

Lambert is an active leader in his fraternity, and comes from an upper-middle-class family which lives in a larger city nearby. He drives an expensive sports car and is impressed with the importance of economic security, planning to enter law school. His family has apparently some involvement in their local church, and Lambert himself has appeared in our morning worship once in a while, though he is not a registered member of the congregation. For more than a year he has been dating a popular girl who is a leader in the student government of the same university. He had not entertained thoughts of immediate marriage because of his plans for going to law school. Lambert felt torn now, he said, between a dedication to study in order to achieve the good grades needed for his long-range plans and the necessity for devoting time and energy to dealing with the crisis in his relationship with the girl.

He said he felt crushed and rejected by her action. He is anguished over the girl's decision to date an older student to whom she had taken a liking in preference to him, although Lambert himself, on becoming aware of this, had insisted on her making a choice. He had telephoned her constantly during the past two weeks, even interrupting her three times during an important sorority meeting, in an effort to win her back or to force her into making a decision about him. Now that she has chosen to date the older student, Lambert is mystified about what she can see in that other man. He suspects her to be sexually involved with the other student, for he knows, he said, that she is spending considerable time in his apartment.

Lambert described his own sexual involvement with the girl for nearly a year. His intercourse with her had been based on his deep love for her. He had taken strong initiative in the beginning, and her cooperation had only come later. He now feels that if the sexual intimacy did not stem from mutual love that would have led to marriage, it must have been based on an illusion and would not have been the "good thing" to do. He recalled an incident when he had come back to see his girl late one summer evening. They had fallen passionately into each other's arms the moment they met, had driven out in his car to a secluded place, and had intercourse. With considerable emotion he described how, afterward, she had sobbed uncontrollably for a long time. He had felt "dirty" about the sexual relationship; he had deceived himself and "offended God." He had gone out into the field by himself and prayed desperately about the matter for an hour, without coming to any peace about it.

Lambert's coming to see me, though he had only a nominal acquaintance with me, suggested that he felt the need to get a religious or pastoral perspective on his problem. My intuition was confirmed by the emotional intensity with which he alluded to a sense of sin about the exploitative character of his sexual relationship. I tried to help Lambert clarify his deep feelings and thoughts, starting by discussing the impact of the girl's rejection on his feelings of self-worth. We explored the possibility that though premarital sexual intercourse was the "in" thing on campus, he himself seemed to feel deep down that it was not the right thing for him to do. He felt guilty over having pressed the girl into sexual intimacy, and suspected that his sexual aggressiveness had undermined the love and respect which had been part of their previous relationship. Could the girl have felt that she was treated as a sex object only, and not as a precious human being who is a child of God? Lambert increasingly expressed his regret over this aspect of his behavior; later in the conversation he came close to confessing the sinfulness of it, seemingly groping for a theological interpretation of his attitudes. He did, however, come through with a clear sense of repentance and regret, not only over his past action but with a movement toward deciding to act differently in the future.

In view of Lambert's nascent sense of sin and repentance it seemed less appropriate to remind him explicitly of God's forgiving grace than to assure him of God's loving providential care for the whole of his life. He picked this up by dwelling on the positive elements of his friendship with the girl, as if to contrast his feeling of uncleanliness with feelings of gratitude. I reminded him that the path to a new harmony with God and to a new sense of cleanness and respect for himself consisted not merely in regretting the past, but more importantly, in resolving not to let his sexual aggressiveness undermine future relationships. This part of the discussion had a calming effect on Lambert, suggesting that clarity about his wrongdoing was less threatening than leaving his thoughts and feelings in a diffuse, bewildering state.

Though Lambert spoke of a personal faith, to which his praying in the field testified, it was essentially a very privatistic dimension of his life. If his faith had been shared in greater communion with others, he might have been helped to envisage more fully the social implications of that faith. As it was, Lambert seemed to find his primary sense of communion in secular form, with his fraternity brothers. But in seeking pastoral help, he also acted on some longing to restore a bond with other believers, perhaps even to place himself under their spiritual guardianship in order to maintain his basic values.

His current crisis highlighted a profound disjunction in his values, however. Though he had some sense of awe and respect for a God to whom he could turn in personal prayer, and whom he could approach through a pastor, he had considerable awe of himself. His view of life was strongly self-centered, and in his relations to others he seemed bent on seeking mostly his own satisfactions.

I prayed with him, recognizing our human need to love and be loved, our powerful sexual passions, our temptations to selfishness, our ability to learn from mistakes, and God's forgiveness and help in relating ourselves to other persons in humane ways. We had talked for about two hours. Lambert expressed gratefulness for this prayer and in the weeks since this visit has greeted me warmly when we met by chance. He has appeared twice at church worship.

I think that Lambert's search for pastoral light on his problem gave him some degree of liberation from bondage to his selfishness and helped set him on the way toward a more promising future, with greater sensitivity to others as well as himself. But he still has a considerable wilderness to travel.

CASE 2: ELIZABETH, AN ACUTELY UNCOMFORTABLE "ADULTERESS" REFERRED BY HER PSYCHIATRIST

Although I have known Elizabeth for some time as a visitor to my church, the pastoral contact she sought with me came at the behest of her psychiatrist. She is a woman in her mid-twenties with attractive appearance, from a rural church background and with a college education. Earlier, when she was working to help her husband get through graduate school, their preschool daughter was enrolled in the church's day care center, a contact which also brought the family occasionally to worship.

Elizabeth phoned me at the church one morning, asking for an appointment to visit about "an important personal problem." When we met the next day, she explained that a divorce, initiated some time ago by her husband, had become final, and that she was now seeing a psychiatrist in order to help her through the process of adjustment. She is pursuing additional college study in order to qualify for work to support herself and her daughter, of whom she has custody. Currently, she finds it difficult to concentrate on her studies, to fall asleep at night, and to make plans for her future. She feels burdened with an overwhelming sense of guilt, which has a paralyzing effect on her whole life. No matter how hard she has tried, she cannot free herself from the power of these guilt feelings, and her psychiatrist had suggested that she discuss this aspect of her situation with a minister. I felt all the more encouraged by this referral to engage Elizabeth in pastoral conversation with a definite religious focus.

Elizabeth made no secret of the fact that she held herself blameworthy for the divorce. When her parents attempted to blame her ex-husband for it, she had told them the truth, namely, that she had had an affair with another man which was the real cause of the marriage failure. Though she and her ex-husband had enjoyed a fairly good marriage, his preoccupation with his studies had left her very lonely and vulnerable to the attentions of a married man with whom she worked. She felt that this affair was morally wrong and that it had brought about the painful consequences she now suffered. She felt she had "sinned against God," deserved to be punished, and needed forgiveness but doubted that it could be granted.

I sensed that Elizabeth had ample awareness of God's holiness, and that this intensified her feelings of guilt over her wrongdoing. Her sense of guilt was vivid and powerful, giving her no respite. She assumed the whole responsibility for the marriage failure, in no way sparing herself, even to the point of discounting her ex-husband's part in letting things go as far as they went. She was indeed repentant enough, in fact punishing herself through her sleeplessness and her inner turmoil. So I helped her explore the dimensions of responsibility, her ex-husband's share of it, and the nature of her feelings of sinfulness.

Sensing her inability to accept God's forgiving grace, I felt that the words of a pastor as "man of God" were needed to move her beyond a confession of sin to restoration in grace. I reminded her that faith in God consists not only in doing what is right, but in accepting his personal love of us, no matter what our moral failures are. We remembered that God's sending his Son is the clear sign of his unbreakable love for each person. I retold for her the story of the woman caught in adultery (John 8: 3–11), whom Jesus had not condemned, but set free with the admonition not to sin again. I applied the meaning of this story to her life, saying that although God did not approve her wrongdoing, his final will was for her not to stand condemned but to regain life. I affirmed her in her struggle to find a new life, noting that, if punishment was needed, she had punished herself quite enough already. In view of her sincere regret I assured her that God offered her his gift of total forgiveness in order that she could be free from the power of her sin and guilt feelings, moving into the full life for which she was destined in Christ.

In response to this story, Elizabeth identified herself with the woman caught in adultery, breaking into tears at the assurance of God's will for freedom for her. When she heard pastoral words of forgiveness in terms directly related to the content of her religious faith, coming from a religious authority, she felt relieved and grateful.

It was plain that Elizabeth trusted me, as she had earlier trusted the church's day care center for her daughter. Yet it had been difficult for her to experience a sense of God's providence, his loving care and guidance, in the midst of these painful events in her life. I suspect that her relatively distant relation to a community of faith and love left her inadequate opportunity for experiencing providence through other persons sharing her faith and calling her attention to "the other side of God."

A prayer shared with Elizabeth lifted to God her feeling of overwhelming guilt, thanking him for his power to destroy those oppressive feelings, and to set her free from them. I prayed that she would be filled with a new sense of well-being and the loving and forgiving presence of God in her life. Elizabeth said that she felt greatly relieved and that she deeply appreciated our visit. A week or two later, she and her daughter appeared at worship. Six weeks later, I telephoned her to see how she was doing. She stated that she was getting along much better, and that the visit had been very helpful.

The fact that this woman was also under psychiatric care and that the psychiatrist had made a specific referral of her to me increased my sense of responsibility as a religious counselor. It enabled me to use my special pastoral resources, even to the point of "proclaiming good tidings" and to seeing her problem, at least in part, as an instance of distorted faith. In essence, Elizabeth "played God" to herself by punishing herself more severely than was, in Christ, demanded.

Case 3: Martha, Bereft and Terrified

Martha is a highly intelligent woman, mother of several grown children, with a long history of depressive states. I have known her for some years as an active member of my church, always willing to help. She sometimes provides child care in her home. She has had two psychiatric hospitalizations, one in her late teens, one a decade ago. Martha is very conscious of her strong tendency to experience emotional highs and lows, mostly the latter. She has drawn upon the support of fellow members of the church and upon my pastoral care in appropriate ways to help her live through her seasons of depression.

Very recently, she lost her husband to death by cancer, after a painful year of intense medical treatment and gradual worsening of the disease. Persons close to Martha, including her parents, feared that her husband's death would precipitate an episode of severe depression. Prior to her husband's death, Martha began to work through her grief, during which time I maintained a close pastoral relation with her.

One morning, two weeks after the death of her husband, I met Martha in the church, where she was doing volunteer work. She was very nervous, appearing to move and act with profound uncertainty, and physically trembling. I invited her into my study for a cup of chocolate and a talk about her condition.

She described her feelings of "being low," saying that these feelings had gradually taken her into a "tailspin" since her husband's death. Things were working out reasonably well in terms of arranging insurance benefits and other business measures; her family loved her, and she felt she had many supportive friends in the church. But despite these supports she could not avoid feeling increasingly overwhelmed by panic. No matter how she tried to reassure herself that things would work out all right, and no matter how realistically she reasoned with herself, the feeling of panic persisted, causing her not to sleep at night and to act and feel nervous all the time.

I asked her about the steps she was taking to try to meet the feelings of panic. She had done two things. She had already made an appointment for that afternoon with her family physician, who knows her medical history, to see about medications that might slow down her emotions. She also had (as I knew) decided to volunteer to help in my church's day care center, as a means of putting her excess nervous energy to work, hoping to find remunerative employment later

Knowing how deeply she felt threatened by her feelings of panic and with how much doom these presented themselves, I tried to look at these with her from the point of view of our shared faith. Could it be that panic, through her past experience with it and its perpetual threat, had become a "holy terror" for her, approaching the status of an idol? As I steered her toward this question, we began to see that she labored under constant temptation to regard the looming panic as an all-powerful "god" who was gaining final control over her life. We recalled together the Bible's view of God as "the God above all the false gods," and how before this true God all lesser gods are idols which are destined eventually to crumble. Martha helped me picture the Bible's vision of faith through the Book of Revelation, in which God is victorious over the monstrous powers of evil.

We recalled Biblical images depicting the final rest, peace, and shalom which come from the hand of the God who is Lord over all. I asked Martha to apply these visions to her life, if she could. She described her life indeed as a situation in which feelings of panic were formidable and quite real, but also expressed some hope that they would finally be crushed under the power of the God in whom she had faith. Her faith, however, needed constant nurture, which she sought in her contacts with other church members in her volunteer work, and which her pastor also should try to give by providing her with a supportive relationship over many years.

Despite her temptation to make an idol of her disposition to depression and give her feelings of panic an almost sacred status, Martha knows her need for communion and has taken active steps to engage in warm give-and-take relations with other people. She knows that being cared for and caring go hand in hand, and on this basis she felt free to visit with me on all occasions when she had acute need for encouragement or consolation. I strongly affirmed the actions she had taken in meeting the threatening panic through volunteer work and seeking her family physician for reasonable medication.

Having to fight off a real threat to her life, Martha also needed to gain hope. Captive as she was to her own feelings of panic and their doom, our conversation helped her see that the strength of these feelings had been partly of her own making—at least she had tended to contribute to their importance by her idolatrous apprehension of them. Increased awareness of the power of God and his ultimate triumph over idols stimulated her hope for a good outcome. She began to see the present threat of panic as a temporary wilderness hardship on the journey toward a more peaceful and healthful life. Our recalling some of the Biblical images of that promised peace helped to strengthen her hope, the force of which could now make her face her situation with some bravery.

In a prayer with her we lifted up her feelings of panic to God, asking that they be destroyed by his power. I asked that his constant presence give Martha a sense of strength and well-being.

Martha seemed reassured and appeared less nervous after our conversation. I have visited briefly with her several times since, and she reports having a tolerable freedom from the feelings of panic. Recently she presided over a meeting in good composure and without undue apprehension. Family members and close friends also report that she is going through this difficult period in her life better than they had dared expect.

I think in this pastoral conversation Martha and I jointly diagnosed a facet of her "disposition" in theological terms as "allowing a false god to rise" by granting her panic undue power and inappropriate holiness. Martha's temptation was to permit an idol to replace the God she believed in, and to feel enslaved. In accentuating the distinctions between God and idols and in describing their impact, one toward freedom, the other toward enslavement, her hope was raised and in proportion to it the panic felt less threatening. The loss of her strong husband intensifies her need for nurture and support in her endeavors to ward off the power that nearly engulfs her. She should be encouraged to continue her active participation in worship, study, fellowship, and service to others; and to continue in personal devotions so as to affirm her identity as a person of faith who is the beloved child of God.

The next report is from a clinically trained, psychiatric hospital chaplain, who typically seeks a pastoral relation with selected individual patients (either at his initiative or by psychiatric referral). He contributes to psychiatric team meetings on diagnosis and treatment. He holds special group meetings with patients, leads occasional worship services, and renders chaplaincy services in the broadest sense within the hospital setting, in constant interaction with members of other mental health disciplines.

CASE 4: BROTHER ANSELM: ABANDONED TO ANGER

In my first meeting with this patient, a brother in a religious order, he told me that he had asked for hospitalization because of his indecisiveness and inability to set priorities, to such a degree that he proved to be dysfunctional at his work. He hoped that one year of hospitalization would allow him a slower pace with less external demands, so that he could get reorganized. It was his desire that his daily world "stop" so that he could get off for one year, and then get back on, better prepared to deal with his world. The patient was raised in a Roman Catholic home and educated in parochial schools. His father abandoned his mother when the patient was an infant, leaving his mother and him in dire financial straits. Later the mother obtained a divorce and remarried. He recalls experiencing some distress and feeling in a dilemma, living with a divorced mother and being taught in church school that divorce is sinful. In high school he did some dating, but recalled returning from a date with the thought, "If that's all there is, then it [the married life] is not for me." After serious and prayerful consideration he elected the religious life as "more growth-producing, more faithful and drawing one closer to God." He acknowledges the desire to be a "beautiful person," like the brothers who taught him, and after three years of religious training he took his vows, and became a teacher in the religious order.

In discussing his vows, at my request, he finds the vow of obedience the most difficult. He understood that vow to mean, "Do what you are told to do, and do not ask for support in doing it." He admits that he became rather rebellious at times, aware of anger at his order for its insensitivity to human need. He is most angry over "ten years of requests for help with emotional problems" which went, by and large, unheeded by his order. The idea of Providence thus obtained a shaky image in his mind. Inclined to talk with me about his "faith problem," he found it difficult to describe in detail what that problem really is. He talked about loss of faith, and of his religious practices being void or empty. While he can teach young people scholastic subjects, albeit with some difficulty, he is sure he could not teach them religion. For he finds himself in the painful position of having invested over fifteen years in a religious vocation, and in commitment to God, who proves to be a god who has abandoned him at his time of greatest need, i.e., his emotional illness. So he felt himself bereft of support from his religious community, his God, and from his family, from which he was emotionally quite distant. Obviously this repeats the abandonment by his father in his infancy.

Long accustomed to an intense prayer life, he finds that praying is now unavailable to him. Prior to his entry into the order, during his high school days, he sometimes cut classes in order to go to church and pray. He thinks his prayer life was always much advanced over the discipline demanded by his order. His prayer was focused on readings on which he would reflect, and then he would pray for guidance in applying the precepts to himself so as to meet the needs of others. His problem with prayer led him to exempt himself from participation in the annual spiritual retreats of his order. Though with effort he can say the rosary, he finds it a "very primitive" form of prayer.

His idea of communion comes through in his thoughts about worship. He now finds it difficult to attend the Eucharist: having been taught to focus all his attention, and bring "all that I am" to the Eucharistic experience, he now finds that he does not know who he is and what he can bring to the liturgy. I asked the patient to outline a form of worship that would be most meaningful to him, and he described a small group of friends meeting in a home where there was silence, meditation, prayerful reflection upon some reading, an exchange of sincere expressions of love and devotion to one another, concluded by a prayer in unison. Asked what would prevent him from engaging in such an experience, even if he himself had to organize it, he spoke of a fear that he could not concentrate enough, or could not bring his "total self" to the event. When I commented that bringing one's total self to a worship experience implies bringing the anger and rage one might have, but that this would also place one in jeopardy for bringing something unacceptable, he said, "Exactly!" with a markedly emotional reaction. "Maybe one of the difficulties is that I have been unwilling to worship *because* I bring so much anger and rage to it."

In the recent past, the patient has begun to explore yoga, Buddhism, and astrology, thinking that these may offer him something that his waning faith cannot now provide. But he feels extremely guilty about these explorations, thinking that he might be spiritually hypocritical. The only significant thing his traditional faith now provides is the part of worship he describes as Holy Communion: "I receive something from it—I guess it is support."

Grace is seen as a reality that all too often seems to have passed him by, due to his repeated experiences of loss. In addition to the sense of loss described earlier, he spoke of having "lost out" on good things in the transition process which his order is going through. In former years he was in religious garb. Later, when the wearing of religious garb went "out of style," he did not have the opportunity to work through the issues of choice with his community. Similarly, in his earlier days the order discouraged "particular relationships," severely disciplining those who transgressed. Now these relationships are permissible, but again he feels that he may have "lost out" on such opportunities. He also feels he "lost out" on transitions in the family. Having been so distant from family living for so many years, he feels he has missed out on some facets of these transitions. More particularly, the death of his stepfather "before I was able to get to know him" is one such loss; in discussing it, the patient wept.

There is a close parallel between the patient's religious experience and his primary family experiences. Just as first his father abandoned him, and then his stepfather before he could get close to him, so his God abandoned him. Just as his religious order promoted (in his view) isolation and distance, so the patient feels isolated and estranged from his family. His search for closeness to a benevolent God and his search for two human fathers have both ended in failure, with pervasive anger and rage. There is a marked absence of significant personal relations now and in his history. Though relationships per se are quite conflicted, his need for them seems at this point keener than his fear of them.

Thus, I recommend a counseling process for this patient with a clinically trained clergyman, to assist him in exploring the significance of his religious practice, and to facilitate his return to healthy expressions of his religious needs in a Christian, Roman Catholic context. The patient's anger and rage must be appropriately expressed toward a clergyman, i.e., in the symbolic presence of his God. Assuming that psychotherapy will continue to be a part of his treatment program, the clergyman who works with him in a counseling relationship must be in frequent contact with the psychotherapist, and be alert to signs of decompensation as well as betterment.

The following report is also from a chaplain. The patient, a woman who had been for some time in a psychiatric hospital, took the initiative in seeking contact with him. Her rather bungling language about herself is at times religious, at times psychiatric, freely mingling these two perspectives as if to imply that she had multi-faceted problems requiring multiple approaches at once.

Case 5: Mrs. Black—Boxed In and Unforgivable

My first contact with Mrs. Black followed the Easter religious service conducted in the hospital. At the end of the service she expressed her appreciation for the opportunity to worship, commenting that religion had meant a great deal to her in her life. She inquired about regular worship services, and expressed some disappointment when I told her that they were held currently only on special occasions. She also stated that she would like to talk with me sometime. After consultation with her hospital physician, it was agreed that I would initiate a series of interviews with her to make some assessment of her personal religious history, her religious concepts, and other life values.

Mrs. Black was raised as a Roman Catholic—her "family church" as she said. First educated in a parochial school with catechetical instruction through the ninth grade, she transferred to a public school in the tenth grade. She regularly attended Mass and other religious activities until she was twelve years old. Her mother took her to church usually, and occasionally her father joined them. Marital problems between mother and father resulted in the mother's dropping church activities, together with her daughter. Mrs. Black resumed a regular attendance pattern when she was fourteen; at eighteen she started college work, and stopped church attendance again.

Upon marrying, she and her husband discussed religious affiliation, mutually agreeing to join The Episcopal Church. Her husband came from a Congregational background with which he was not entirely comfortable, and she, coming from a Roman Catholic background with less than full comfort, thought that Episcopal worship would offer both what they were looking for. For her, the ritual was rather similar, but the new church seemed to have fewer prohibitions. Mr. Black found more formality in the new church, and appreciated it. After college and marriage, Mr. Black went into the Navy, and was stationed at San Diego. The pair continued worshiping at the post chapel. They lived a few doors from the Roman Catholic chaplain, whom they occasionally entertained in their home. Mrs. Black and this chaplain would get into rather extensive discussions of the Roman Catholic Church's stand on such issues as abortion and birth control. Upon her husband's return to civilian life the couple attended Episcopal services, but with increasing irregularity on the husband's part. After the birth of their first child, Mrs. Black stopped church attendance and involvement.

Mrs. Black's faith is caught up in moral polarities. Her attitudes toward life and personal situations are either "good or bad, right or wrong, black or white." She feels this comes directly from her early religious instruction. She was taught that there is no "gray"—things are either white or black. The last time she went to confession was when she was thirteen— she found the priest critical of her for her failure to attend Mass. She left the confessional box in tears because she felt she was held accountable for something over which she had no control, for if her mother did not take her to church, she had no way of getting there.

What is holy for her? It is "God," whom she describes as "an older figure—like a father." Her faith in him is admittedly ambivalent. She believes in him up to a point, finding it difficult to understand why some people find support from him while he seems particularly unavailable to her. She thinks of Jesus Christ as a "holy man," emphasizing his humanity. The personal future is vague to her—she has no idea of "things to come," and is far from sure about any heaven or hell. In these ideas, fragments of her conservative Roman Catholic upbringing come through as well as her unease with them.

Worship, which she likes, seems to be devoid of any sense of communion. She stresses the "good feeling" she gets from it, which seems quite private and may be an aesthetic response, but she also appreciates it morally as "a good thing" to do.

Curiously, she considers being a mother the "greatest Christian act," as if it were a charitable deed. Second in line of Christian acts is "doing things for others." Asked to reflect about sin, she ranked adultery as the greatest sin, and murder as the next greatest, apparently taking sin as specific misdeeds. Significantly, she added that her judgment about murder did not quite include suicide. While she admitted to feeling "not right, or guilty," when contemplating suicide, she stated that she nevertheless keeps the idea of suicide "in the back of my mind" as an option she could take, apparently with little or no repentance.

Her relationships with others are beset with fateful ruminations that seem to belie any relevance of grace or trust in her life. She refers to her mother as a "schizophrenic" and describes herself by the same diagnostic label, feeling that she is doomed to have the same "illness" despite her "knowing logically" that this need not be the case. Suicide would be a way to avoid "passing on the illness to my children."

Her description of her father resembles that of God, an older father figure. Apparently her father spent a great deal of time with her, taking her with him on his jobs. She mentioned with warm affection the opportunity he gave her of naming the various products he manufactured. Yet, while stating that her father "brought me up as a son," she also insisted that she learned more about "being a woman" from her father than from her mother.

Her relationship with her husband is openly conflictual. She feels the conflict stems from competition between them in their business, her husband's stereotype about the role of women, and finally his rejection of her by his pursuit of an extramarital affair. Describing her children as "fine little boys" who are doing fairly well now, she has ominous feelings about their future. She wants to pass on to them a sense of emotional security, but does not know whether she is capable of this. She wants to give them religious instruction, not by didactic means but by transmitting to them "a sense of faith"—but she has little faith herself.

In a word, Mrs. Black has found no deep sense of communion or affiliation, either at home or in her church. But she senses that some "community experience" is developing for her on the hospital ward. Consistent with her positive feelings toward her father and her sense of distance from her mother, she finds it easier to relate to men than women patients.

In general, her relationships lack a conviction of grace, and toward herself she maintains an unforgiving attitude. Extremely sensitive to other people's thoughts or standards, and reluctant to express her own opinion on any issue, she seems caught in a constant fear of rejection. She cannot express anger for fear of receiving hostility in return. Unable to measure up to standards of others or herself, she cannot forgive herself for her failure to measure up. All demands on her are felt as harsh and relentless.

The values she cherishes are motherhood and marriage. The first gives opportunity for molding, teaching, and guiding a young life, and thus represents a high calling, but the patient feels ill prepared for it, and perhaps ambivalent about it. She sees marriage as holy because of the single commitment and fidelity it entails. This is for her pinpointed in sexual intercourse, in which one "gives oneself" to the other. Given these particular values, Mrs. Black finds it extremely difficult to even think about divorce. She feels truly "boxed in," stating, "My husband almost drove me nuts, but I can't divorce him." Though she thought about an extramarital affair in order to retaliate against her husband, she found herself unable to initiate this for she could not live with herself if she did. Feeling helpless, unforgiven, guilty, and weary she is almost convinced that she will never be free of illness.

Somewhat dramatic and seductive in these interviews, the patient seemed to be at ease in discussing religious concepts. At first she externalized her problems—they seemed to depend on "whether God was really out there or not," or whether there is a hereafter, and she sought the cause of her disturbance in her mother and husband. Thus what made her ill was her mother, her husband, and her religion. But in later interviews she was able also to consider internal reasons for her disturbance.

In many respects, religion had played a dominant role in her development, but it appears unintegrated and conflict-laden. I recommend pastoral counseling for this patient to give her an opportunity to review religious ideas so as to integrate some and reject others. Ideas that need attention are forgiveness, fellowship, sin, suffering, and worship. In light of her catechetical training, the absence of felt forgiveness and a sense of church fellowship is striking.

Several afterthoughts occur at this point. In the case reports presented, the writers make no attempt to round off their diagnostic observations and inferences into a capsule phrase or label, as one is accustomed to find in medical and psychiatric case reports. Should they have made such an attempt?

On several grounds, I do not think so. In the first place, pastoral thought is not medical thought. Medicine is focused on diseases and the distinctions between kinds of disease; psychiatry, for better or worse, has long been in the habit of finding suitable analogues of the medical concept of disease for classifying the malfunctions that come its way. Psychiatry's efforts in this direction have been fraught with theoretical and practical problems. In recognition of these a number of alternative conceptions have been proposed, such as stress reactions, adaptation syndromes, personality disturbances, character styles, coping patterns, or learning disorders. Many of these better conceptions have in turn led to new diagnostic labels, as if to suggest that there are discrete units of psychiatric dysfunction. Whether or not this be so, the kinds of problems for which persons seek pastoral help defy classification grafted on any disease model. I see no virtue in pastoral one-word diagnoses (analogous to *appendicitis* or *hysteria*) that emulate medical or psychiatric habits of classifying.

Though medieval moral theology did produce one-word designations for conditions of man (e.g., "acedia") suggestive of discrete entities, this nomenclature derived from conceptions of sin, concretized in lists of vices, as opposed to virtues. I think that modern theological thought would rather take an altogether different approach, one that is a priori loath to classify and pigeonhole people in terms of *any* categorical system. The subject of pastoral theology is the person, the concrete man, woman, or child and his personal interactions, not a disease, disorder, vice, deviation, or defect. Attuned as it is to personal states of being and personal journeys of becoming, modern pastoral theology requires in its practice a personalistic language that can capture experiences, events, outlooks, struggles, attitudes, feelings, hopes, and the values that men live by. This demands narration and leads to descriptive vignettes which capture a style of living or an existential posture, perhaps even in the form of dramatic episodes.

For all these reasons, I rejoice in the narrations and experiential phrases of the preceding reports and have no chagrin over the absence of capsules of classification. I hope indeed that the latter will never be proposed.

A second thought pertains to the contributions these reports make to interdisciplinary or transdisciplinary understanding of the parishioners or patients. In cases 4 and 5, the written pastoral reports were eventually read by members of various mental health professions—psychiatrists, psychologists, social workers, nurses, or others. Upon my inquiry (which was not instigated by the chaplains who wrote these reports), these other specialists invariably said that they appreciated the reports as written. The text forced them to think of similarities and differences, parallels, analogues, confirmations, contradictions, or surprising novelties between their own data and these pastoral data. In the two hospital patients, moreover, the interdisciplinary assessment and recommendations led to an adequate division of therapeutic labor in which several modalities of intervention took place alongside each other, reinforcing each other so as to achieve the best overall progress.

Thirdly, it is apparent that the writing of these reports and the conducting of the interviews which they reflect have helped these pastors to be aware of their professional integrity and sensitive to the unique relationship they engaged in with their charges. Looking at the other side of the pastoral relationship, neither the word "patient" nor the word "client" adequately describes the role the problem-laden persons themselves assumed vis-à-vis these pastors. Some might have been patients of a hospital or at some time clients of a social agency. However, they were something quite different in their interviews with these pastors. For want of a better term I used the word "charges" in a previous sentence. This word captures something of the shepherding function which is part of the pastoral office, but unfortunately it does not describe the attitude or role which the help-seeking person assumes in this relationship to the pastors. Another word I have used and which I favor is "parishioner," but it has implications of registered church membership which do not always hold.

In the first case, the person was a casual visitor to the pastor's church. In the second case, the pastor was sought out by a member of his congregation at the suggestion of a psychiatrist in private practice, whom she also saw. The third case is an episode in a long-established pastoral relationship with a congregant who needs periodically special pastoral

help. In the fourth case, a pastoral consultation was asked by
the hospital's psychiatric team leader for a patient who was
pledged to a religious vocation, a fact which may have led to
a sense of collegiality in the relationship between this brother
and the chaplain. In the fifth case, a hospital patient
initiated contact with the chaplain, thereby exercising her
freedom to use him as a special resource for obtaining some
light on her problems, if not her being. To do this did not
make her a patient, client, patron, customer, ward, pupil,
parishioner, or anything else reminiscent of a definable social
role vis-à-vis the pastor (chaplain) she sought out. I am
pressing this point about nomenclature to prepare us to
envision the possibility that the concept of *role* may at times
be out of order in describing the working relations between a
person and his or her pastor.

If pastoral work is seen as a profession, it calls for definable
role behaviors between the interacting parties. But if it is
seen as a calling, the agapic community, which I described in
Chapter IX as one wellspring of pastoral care, adds other
features which transcend the role concept. What is true for
the pastor should then also be true for the person seeking his
help: he or she claim this help as friend, person, child of God,
believer, or "soul in need"—as participant in a communion
that transcends all partitions and divisions.

NOTES

1. Jean-Paul Sartre, *Nausea*, tr. by Lloyd Alexander (New Directions, 1949).

2. Alfred North Whitehead, *Adventures of Ideas* (The Macmillan Company, 1933).

3. Alfred North Whitehead, *Process and Reality: An Essay in Cosmology* (The Macmillan Company, 1929).

4. William James, *Psychology: Briefer Course* (Henry Holt & Company, 1892), p. 29.

5. Paul W. Pruyser, "The Use and Neglect of Pastoral Resources," *Pastoral Psychology*, Vol. XXIII (1972), pp. 5–17.

6. Talcott Parsons, "Belief, Unbelief and Disbelief," in Rocco Caporale and Antonio Grumelli (eds.), *The Culture of Unbelief* (University of California Press, 1971), pp. 215–216 and ff.

7. *Malleus Maleficarum*, tr. by Montague Summers (London: Pushkin Press, 1951).

8. Jonathan Edwards, *A Treatise Concerning Religious Affections* (1746), new edition, ed. by John E. Smith, in *The Works of Jonathan Edwards*, Vol. II, ed. by Perry Miller (Yale University Press, 1959).

9. For Søren Kierkegaard's "diagnostic" works, see especially:
    Either/Or, tr. by David F. and Lillian M. Swenson (Princeton University Press, 1944).

    Stages on Life's Way, tr. by Walter Lowrie (Princeton University Press, 1940)

The Concept of Dread, tr. by Walter Lowrie (Princeton University Press, 1944).

The Sickness Unto Death, tr. by Walter Lowrie (Princeton University Press, 1941).

10. Paul W. Pruyser, "The Minister as Diagnostician," *The Perkins School of Theology Journal,* Vol. XXVII (1973), pp. 1–10. This article gives a list of the books on pastoral care and counseling inspected for evidence of diagnostic thought.

11. Edgar Draper, *Psychiatry and Pastoral Care* (Prentice-Hall, Inc. 1965).

12. Seward Hiltner, *Preface to Pastoral Theology* (Abingdon Press, 1958), pp. 98–113; and *Religion and Health* (The Macmillan Company, 1943).

13. John T. McNeill, *A History of the Cure of Souls* (Harper & Brothers, 1951).

14. Boisen's approach to the hospital chaplaincy and his relative unease with later developments in the clinical pastoral education movement are best described, though cryptically, in his autobiography: Anton Boisen: *Out of the Depths* (Harper & Brothers, 1960), Ch. V, "An Adventure in Theological Education," pp. 143–197.

15. Anton Boisen, *Lift Up Your Hearts: A Service-Book for Use in Hospitals* (Pilgrim Press, 1926); later retitled *Hymns of Hope and Courage* (Pilgrim Press, 1932, 1950).

16. The statements in the text regarding the influence of Carl Rogers on pastoral counseling refer specifically to his two earlier books which achieved wide circulation: Carl R. Rogers, *Counseling and Psychotherapy: Newer Concepts in Practice* (Houghton Mifflin Company, 1942) and *Client-Centered Therapy: Its Current Practice, Implications, and Theory* (Houghton Mifflin Company, 1951).

17. Finer points of my criticism of the allegedly "humanist" movement in clinical psychology can be found in the following article: Paul W. Pruyser, "The Beleaguered Individual: Images of Man in Clinical Practice," *Bulletin of the Menninger Clinic,* Vol. XXXVII (1973), pp. 433–450.

18. L. Jackson and J. Haag, "Attitudes Toward Chaplaincy: A Survey of Attitudes of Patients and Staff Toward the Role of Chaplain in a Psychiatric Hospital" (Menninger School of Psychiatry, Graduation Paper, 1974).

E. S. Golden, "What Influences the Role of the Protestant Chaplain in an Institutional Setting?" *Journal of Pastoral Care*, Vol. XVI (1962), pp. 218–225.

M. D. Gynther and J. O. Kempson, "Attitudes of Mental Patients and Staff Toward a Chaplaincy Program," *Journal of Pastoral Care*, Vol. XIV (1960), pp. 211–217.

W. Knights and D. Kramer, "The Role of the Chaplain in Mental Hospitals," in E. Mansell Pattison (ed.), *Clinical Psychiatry and Religion* (Little, Brown & Company, 1969), pp. 257–267.

19. The following paragraphs in this chapter draw on observations and inferences first made in my paper: Paul W. Pruyser, "Assessment of the Patient's Religious Attitudes in the Psychiatric Case Study," *Bulletin of the Menninger Clinic*, Vol. XXXV (1971), pp. 272–291. A briefer German translation appeared as "Die Erhebung von religiösen Einstellungen des Patienten in der psychiatrischen Fallstudie," *Wege zum Menschen*, Vol. XXV (1973), pp. 403–415.

20. Quoted from Jackson and Haag, *loc. cit.*

21. T. W. Klink, unpublished case study, Topeka State Hospital.

22. Thomas S. Szasz, *The Myth of Mental Illness: Foundations of a Theory of Personal Conduct* (1961), rev. ed. (Harper & Row, Publishers, Inc., 1974), and *The Manufacture of Madness: A Comparative Study of the Inquisition and the Mental Health Movement* (Harper & Row, Publishers, Inc., 1970).

23. Karl Menninger, Martin Mayman, and Paul W. Pruyser, *The Vital Balance* (The Viking Press, Inc., 1963) and *A Manual for Psychiatric Case Study*, 2d ed. (Grune & Stratton, Inc., 1962).

24. Paul W. Pruyser, *A Dynamic Psychology of Religion* (Harper & Row, Publishers, Inc., 1968), and *Between Belief and Unbelief* (Harper & Row, Publishers, Inc., 1974).

25. Friedrich Schleiermacher, *Über die Religion: Reden an die Gebildeten unter ihren Verächtern* (1799), tr. by John Oman as *On Religion* (Frederick Ungar Publishing Company, 1955).

26. Rudolf Otto, *Das Heilige* (1917), tr. by John W. Harvey as *The Idea of the Holy* (Oxford University Press, 1928).

27. E. Jones, "Psycho-analysis and the Christian Religion," in

Essays in Applied Psycho-analysis, Vol. II (London: Hogarth Press, Ltd., 1951), p. 203.

28. Gabriel Marcel, *Homo Viator: Introduction to a Metaphysic of Hope*, tr. by Emma Crawford (Henry Regnery Co., 1951). Paul W. Pruyser, "Phenomenology and Dynamics of Hoping," *Journal for the Scientific Study of Religion*, Vol. III (1963), pp. 86–97.

29. Jean-Paul Sartre, *Being and Nothingness: An Essay on Phenomenological Ontology*, tr. by Hazel E. Barnes (Philosophical Library, Inc., 1956).

30. Paul Tillich, *The Courage to Be* (Yale University Press, 1952).

31. William James, *The Will to Believe, and Other Essays in Popular Philosophy* (Longmans, Green & Company, Inc., 1897).

32. Paul W. Pruyser, "The Master Hand," in William B. Oglesby, Jr. (ed.), *The New Shape of Pastoral Theology: Essays in Honor of Seward Hiltner* (Abingdon Press, 1969).

33. Eric Hoffer, *The True Believer: Thoughts on the Nature of Mass Movements* (Harper & Brothers, 1951).

34. Seward Hiltner, *Preface to Pastoral Theology* (Abingdon Press, 1958), p. 108.

35. Studs Terkel, *Working: People Talk About What They Do All Day and How They Feel About What They Do* (Pantheon Books, 1974).

36. Quoted from Oskar Pfister, *Christianity and Fear* (London: George Allen & Unwin, Ltd., 1948), p. 26.

37. For a few noteworthy examples of these trends in analytic and linguistic philosophy and the religious defense they have elicited, see:

    Alfred J. Ayer, *Language, Truth and Logic* (1936)
      (Dover Publications, 1946).

    George E. Moore, *Philosophical Studies*
      (London: Kegan Paul, 1922).

    Ian T. Ramsey, *Religious Language*
      (London: SCM Press, Ltd., 1957).

    Gilbert Ryle, *The Concept of Mind*
      (London: Hutchinson's University Library, 1949).

    Gilbert Ryle, *Dilemmas*
      (Cambridge: Cambridge University Press, 1954).

Ludwig Wittgenstein, *Philosophische Untersuchungen,* tr.
by G. E. M. Anscombe as *Philosophical Investigations*
(Oxford: Basil Blackwell & Mott, Ltd., 1953).

38. Erik H. Erikson, "Eight Ages of Man," in *Childhood and Society,* 2d ed. (W. W. Norton & Company, 1963), pp. 247–274.

39. Harvey Cox, *Feast of Fools* (Harvard University Press, 1969).

INDEX